Arts: A Third Level Course

The Development of Instruments and their Music
Units 12–13

The Rise of the Symphony 1

Prepared by Dinah Barsham for the Course Team

The Open University Press

The Open University Press
Walton Hall, Milton Keynes.

First published 1974.

Copyright © 1974 The Open University.

All rights reserved. No part of this work may be reproduced in any form, by mimeograph or any other means, without permission in writing from the publisher.

Designed by the Media Development Group of the Open University.

Printed in Great Britain by
Martin Cadbury, a specialized division of Santype International,
Worcester and London.

ISBN 0 335 00856 9

This text forms part of an Open University course. The complete list of units in the course appears at the end of this text.

For general availability of supporting material referred to in this text, please write to the Director of Marketing, The Open University, P.O. Box 81, Walton Hall, Milton Keynes, MK7 6AA.

Further information on Open University courses may be obtained from the Admissions Office, The Open University, P.O. Box 48, Walton Hall, Milton Keynes, MK7 6AA.

CONTENTS

1	Preamble	5
2	The origins of the symphony	6
3	Musical establishments and centres	14
4	Education	32
5	Performance practice	36
6	Technological development and orchestration	38
7	Some terms relating to style	47
8	Early symphonies and symphonists	49
9	How to read a score	51
10	Case Study 1	53
11	Case Study 2	57
12	Case Study 3	62
13	Case Study 4	67
14	Case Study 5	71
15	Case Study 6	76
	Appendix	84

1.0 PREAMBLE

1.1 This music course examines a number of areas of development, both musical and technical, and traces cross-influences and growth within them. In these units we are going to explore an area of relatively uncharted musical territory[1]: that surrounding the origins and early years of what we now know as the Classical symphony. The Classical symphony of Haydn, Mozart, Beethoven and Schubert is familiar in style, form, orchestration and general characteristics, and we can read about the cultural and social conditions under which these composers and their contemporaries lived and worked. However, stylistic and formal developments in the early history of the symphony between, say, the 1730s and 1770s are not so familiar to us. Neither even are the names of many of the composers who contributed to the symphony's growth. In exploring this area we are concerned also with technological development and the influence and taste of the growing new class of audience and patron, whose satisfaction and approval at public concerts provided a continual demand for such new works as symphonies.

1.2 These units will examine the environment and conditions out of which the early symphony emerged and then look at six examples as case studies of the way in which the new musical style was fostered in different centres. The three early symphonic movements are by Sammartini (before 1744, Milan), Wagenseil (1746, Vienna) and Stamitz (1750s, Mannheim), and the three complete symphonies from the next generation of symphony composers are by C. P. E. Bach (1775, Hamburg), J. C. Bach (1781, London) and Rosetti (1787, Wallerstein). These pieces, all illustrated on the accompanying gramophone record, have been chosen to try to show the contribution that was made by important composers from different musical centres and different stylistic and formal traditions. You will notice that the last three case studies were written during the years when both Haydn and Mozart were themselves producing symphonies. This is because I think it is important that you should be aware of the contemporary achievements out of which Haydn and Mozart each emerged to stand head and shoulders above their fellow composers. The block will be accompanied by two television programmes. The first, *The Mannheim Sound*, aims to identify features which made the music written at this outstanding musical centre and the way it was played unique, and the second concerns interpretation. There is a radio programme, *Stylistic Change from Baroque to Classical*, illustrated by musical extracts; and an appendix listing the contents of the disc, the names of early symphony composers with their places of employment, and commercial gramophone records currently available. The third unit of the block contains musical scores of the case studies. There is an assignment associated with these units, and the work contained in them is intended to occupy three weeks.

1.3 I am grateful to the A304 Course Team for constructive criticism and continuous advice and suggestions during the writing of these units. Charles Cudworth acted as specialist consultant for them, and his expert knowledge of the period was invaluable to me. John Rutter made the orchestral scores from original manuscripts and early editions, and helped in the preparation of orchestral parts for the recording sessions. Barrie Jones gathered together the information for the appendix. Nevertheless, I accept overall responsibility for the block.

---

[1] As this unit went to press, there appeared Vol. VII of the New Oxford History of Music, *The Age of Enlightenment 1745–1790*, ed. Egon Wellesz and Frederick Sternfeld containing 'The Early Symphony'.

1.4 However much we talk about the various influences that contributed to the development of the classical symphony, it is not until we look at some early works in detail that we can best understand and appreciate the achievements of the early symphonists. The core of these units, therefore, is the case studies, which I hope will give you an awareness of the stylistic, orchestral and structural experiments tried out on the audiences of the eighteenth century, who appear to have received them with appreciation and enthusiasm. First I want to consider some peripheral aspects that set the historical, social and musical picture. It is not necessary to memorize names and details mentioned concerning musical centres and education, which are included to give a general picture. However, I should hope that you would remember facts concerning the origins of the symphony, its changing form and style and the way in which the symphony orchestra developed.

2.0 THE ORIGINS OF THE SYMPHONY

2.1 The story of the emergence of the symphony as an established form is a complex one. It concerns not only the evolution of the form, but also the emergence of Classical musical language from the Baroque idiom of the early part of the century. By musical language I mean the texture, pattern of harmonic movement, nature and shape of melodies, disposition of melodic and accompanying parts and so on. Professor J. P. Larsen, the Danish musicologist, in his paper *Some Observations on the Development and Characteristics of Vienna Classical Instrumental Music*[1] describes the essential features of Classical music as:

> the equal importance of formal and expressive features, the synthesis of homophonic and polyphonic approach, the consummation of about 200 years' development of 'functional' harmony and tonality, the striving for clarity, the balancing of design and colour, the combination of fixed and graduated dynamics and still a number of [even more] features.

Some of the differences of style between Baroque and Classical can be clearly seen from even a casual comparison of two examples of score, the first from one of Bach's Brandenburg Concertos (1721) and the second from Mozart's Piano Concerto in A major (K 488, 1786).

---

[1] *Studio Musicologica Academiae Scientiarum Hungaricae* 9, 1967.

J. S. Bach: Concerto No. 3

Mozart: Piano Concerto in A major K 488

You can see at once that the whole concept of the music is different. In the Bach example everybody is busy all the time. All the parts are equally weighted and equally important. The mood is set and stays that way. The Mozart extract is precisely and exactly scored in a more selective and economical way. The tune is of supreme importance and the accompaniment is sensitive and expressive. Touches of chromaticism (accidentals) add subtlety to an apparently simple tune and its accompaniment. It is highly personal.

2.2 During the first half of the eighteenth century by far the most popular form in orchestral music was the concerto. As the century progressed opera symphonies or overtures, or incidental music, also became regular concert items. These opera overtures are obvious predecessors of the symphony. At this time they were composed either in the French form with a slow introduction followed by a fugal allegro which is rounded off by a broader coda (occasionally extended into a third movement) or in the Italian form, fast-slow-fast. Indeed, the terms overture (French derivation) and symphony (Italian derivation) were at this time synonymous. And soon, with the growing popularity of the form, these opera symphonies were composed without reference to any opera. It was not only as concert items that symphonies became popular, however. Charles Burney[1] reports an unexpected setting for a symphony performance in Turin.

> In the chapel there is commonly a symphony played every morning between eleven and twelve o'clock, by the King's band, which is divided into three orchestras, and placed in three different galleries: and though far separated from each other, the performers know their business so well that there is no want of a person to beat time, as in the opera and Concert Spirituel at Paris. The King, the royal family, and the whole city seem very constant in their attendance at mass; and on commondays all their devotion is silently performed at the Messa Bassa, during the symphony. On festivals Signor Pugnani plays a solo, or the Besozzis a duet, and sometimes motets are performed with voices. The organ is in the gallery which faces the king, and in this stands the principal first violin.

2.3 Each of our first three case studies represents an important, developing style. It is clear that influences and reputations travelled fast and widely during the eighteenth century, and by the time the later case studies were composed we

---

[1] Dr Charles Burney (traveller, writer, musician and historian): *The Present State of Music in France and Italy*, 1771.

can see assimilation and integration of a variety of elements. Later in this unit, when I try to define some of the names that are given to the many styles of this period, the question arises as to whether it was the Austro-German national facility to adopt and develop the best of foreign styles that led to Vienna becoming the home of the Classical symphony.

2.4 There were many important 'schools' of symphony composers—the Italian school, the Viennese school, the Mannheim school, the North German school and the Paris and London schools in particular. But I should stress the point that nearly all our knowledge and conclusions are based on the study of Western European music, and that a vast repertoire of mid-European orchestral music is practically unknown to us in the West. It seems that composers were well informed about each other however, and, when they were able, travelled abroad to direct their own works. Dissemination of new ideas and styles was widespread. For example, the new modern elements of the Mannheim style were brought over to England by the Earl of Kelly, who, Dr Burney[1] informs us:

> travelled into Germany . . . shut himself up at Mannheim with the elder Stamitz [There were three important Stamitz's. This one, Johann, was the father], and studied composition and practised the violin with such serious application that, at his return to England, there was no part of theoretical or practical Music in which he was not equally versed with the greatest professors [This term, here used in the eighteenth-century sense, means 'professional'] of his time. Indeed, he had a strength of hand on the violin, and a genius for composition, with which few professors are gifted.

Lord Kelly then proceeded to publish symphonies in a similar style to Stamitz (in fact Charles Cudworth[2] considers that some are too similar for coincidence) and did much to foster the new ideas and developments from the continent. Many of the musicians at Mannheim were of Bohemian origin and brought with them elements characteristic of their homeland—dance rhythms, vitality and *joie de vivre*. Jommelli, one of the strongest influences in the early development of the symphony, was an eminent Italian working amid musicians of varied nationalities at the court of Charles Eugène of Württembêrg. The strong Protestant tradition of North Germany percolated into the symphony through J. S. Bach's son C. P. E. Bach, who lived and worked in Berlin and Hamburg.

2.5 It is popularly said that the symphony was 'born' at Mannheim. Certainly the musical establishment there, gathered together by Duke Carl Theodor, consisted of an extraordinarily gifted group of musicians—performers and composers. That most of these musicians were imported from Bohemia, Austria and Italy proves that the style of composition and performance at Mannheim was by no means indigenous but nurtured over many years by the working conditions and stimulus of the Mannheim environment. As Burney tells us:[3]

> It was here [at Mannheim] that Stamitz, stimulated by the productions of Jom(m)elli [at Stuttgart] first surpassed the bounds of common opera overtures, which had hitherto only served in the theatre as a kind of court crier, into an 'O Yes!' in order to awaken attention and bespeak silence, at the entrance of the singers. Since the discovery which the genius of Stamitz first made, every effect has been tried which such an aggregate

[1] Charles Burney, *History of Music*.
[2] C. L. Cudworth, *English Eighteenth-century Symphonies*, Royal Musical Association, 1952.
[3] Charles Burney, *The Present State of Music in Germany*.

of sound can produce; it was here that the *Crescendo* and *Diminuendo* had birth;[1] and the *Piano*, which was before chiefly used as an echo, with which it was generally synonymous, as well as the *Forte*, were found to be musical *colours* which had their *shades*, as much as red or blue in painting.

However, it is not only for their excellence of ensemble, bowing, dynamics, phrasing and so on that the Mannheimers have remained important. It is because the Mannheim composers, and in particular Johann Stamitz, their first leader, firmly established and stabilized a new orchestral form and idiom in the symphony. Their orchestral playing, with all its subtleties, was merely the means of interpreting and faithfully performing their new style of composition. Of course, parallel and equally important developments were being made at other musical centres, but Mannheim was certainly important in its tradition and influence, and it is hard to resist the glamour that appears to have surrounded it.

2.6 Early symphonies, in three or four movements, were simple and unsophisticated in form. Here is the first movement of an early symphony by Stamitz.

Stamitz: Symphony in G (*c.* 1745)

[1] Burney's accuracy here is questionable.

Exercise

From your experience of Baroque music, and judging from a brief look on paper:

1 What form is this in?
2 What is characteristic about the instrumental layout?

Discussion

I expect you recognized (1) the familiar Baroque two-part binary form, and (2) the characteristic importance of the outer parts (that is, the steadily moving bass part and the melodic interest confined to the upper violin parts).

Compare this with the score of the Stamitz first movement of your case study.

This movement is all of one piece and obviously in a more ambitious form. A fuller orchestra is required and woodwind and horns have written-out, fully independent parts of their own. The page abounds in dynamic and performance marks, and it is obvious that every note is thought and written for a specific instrument. **Play the recording of this movement a couple of times.** The movement as a whole has a drive and purpose—a sort of inevitability. This is due to Stamitz's most important development—that of the internal organization of a movement. His first movements, and those of other Mannheimers, began to establish a definite, though primitive, sonata form. A100 students may remember that we discussed this most basic and influential of the developmental forms in the Arts Foundation Course, Units 15 and 16, *Form and Meaning*. In fact the plan employed by the early symphonists (around 1740) was a simplified version, originally like this:

|| : I (tonic) – II (dominant) : || : I (dominant) – I (tonic) – II tonic : ||

which by the time of our case study around the 1750s was more like this (remember the Mannheimers were experimenters!)

I a, b, c (tonic) – II (dominant) – Brief development – I a, b, c and II in any possible order (tonic)

This plan relies for its satisfaction, both to the composer and the listener, on the contrast of key and thematic material stated, the organic development of stated themes in a development section and the recapitulation of the original material in the home key. And this brings us to one of the biggest differences between a Baroque and Classical working-out, the organic nature of development. A Baroque motif or theme does not change essentially during the course of a movement. A Classical theme, however, must be constructed so that it is still recognizable even when changed extensively. In his book *Classic and Romantic Music*, Professor F. Blume says of a theme for development:

> The motif must remain undisturbed in its essential characteristics when it is transposed into various keys, combined at will with others, given different colour, articulation, rhythm, or when, the rhythm remaining the same, it gives rise to a different melody, is differently harmonized, when it is inverted, lengthened, shortened—and it must be suited to all such transmogrifications. . . .

It would seem, perhaps, that the secret of the developmental forms lies in the construction of new sorts of themes, which are capable of development. Stamitz and Wagenseil, both of whom are represented in the case studies, are each important for the way their themes are constructed of shorter motifs.

Developmental form, and more specifically sonata form, gives satisfaction to the composer in that it gives him the opportunity to develop ideas in every way, melodically, rhythmically, harmonically and orchestrally, before rounding the movement off with a re-statement of the original material. It affords the listener satisfaction since he is able to recognize the development of the motifs or themes he has heard in the exposition, and he is also able to appreciate the harmonic movement and surprises that occur in the development before the composer manoeuvres into position for the recapitulation. And he also appreciates the changed link or bridge passage between the first and second subjects which gives the tonal satisfaction of ending up in the home key. It's fairly clear that Haydn's audiences, for example, could follow what was happening, since he plays deliberate tricks on them, side-stepping obvious tonalities in a recapitulation and so on; today's audience have heard so much more music, from earlier and later periods, in which tonality is less well defined, that it is unlikely that such sophistications are generally appreciated. The whole system is open to all sorts of amendments, improvements and extensions.

Stamitz firmly established the sections of this sonata-form in a way that others were able to improve upon and refine. His opening themes are bold and vigorous, his secondary themes fully-fledged and contrasting. His contribution in this way is considerable. Although he was not the first to introduce it (members of the Viennese school possibly were), the four-movement plan seems to have been satisfactorily established at Mannheim, but whether the third movement was inserted or the fourth movement added is a matter for conjecture.

2.7 The years in between 1740 and the 1780s saw the production of a great many three- and four-movement symphonies by composers in Germany, Austria, Italy, France and England. Cross-fertilization of ideas was due to a large extent to the great mobility of musicians, and the dissemination of new ideas by such travellers and writers as Dr Charles Burney, who did so much to publicize the standards and innovations that he witnessed during his remarkable travels. Before going further into the question of style, form and orchestration, therefore, let's consider the different musical establishments and centres that were encouraging the growth of the symphony during the middle years of the eighteenth century.

3.0 MUSICAL ESTABLISHMENTS AND CENTRES

3.1 During the eighteenth century musical establishments were flourishing throughout Europe. Courts with any pretensions at all had their private theatres, opera houses, chapels and concert rooms and employed as many musicians as they could afford. Italians predominated in the world of opera, both as performers and composers, but in the other fields German, Bohemian and Austrian music began to play an influential role. Here is a map of mid-eighteenth century Europe showing places that were particularly active musically. Below is a brief summary of the musical facilities at some of these centres and also lists of prominent musicians working or visiting there at some time. This information is necessarily somewhat arbitrary, but it gives an idea of the immense popularity of musical entertainment and the productivity of a large number of active composers, who appear to have been reasonably mobile. They moved around, as anyone does nowadays, because they were dissatisfied with a position, or with the musical set-up of an establishment, or to get more money or work with better colleagues or in a more lively musical environment. They were invited to direct musical performances of their works at considerable distances from home, and language or nationality seemed to be no bar to communication. Reputations must have travelled widely. I mention these musicians and statistics merely to give an impression of the wealth of music and musicians in circulation, and it is certainly not necessary to remember details. I hope it does, however, serve to exemplify what kind of activity was going on at the time. I have put musicians who were not indigenous, and visited only briefly, in square brackets.

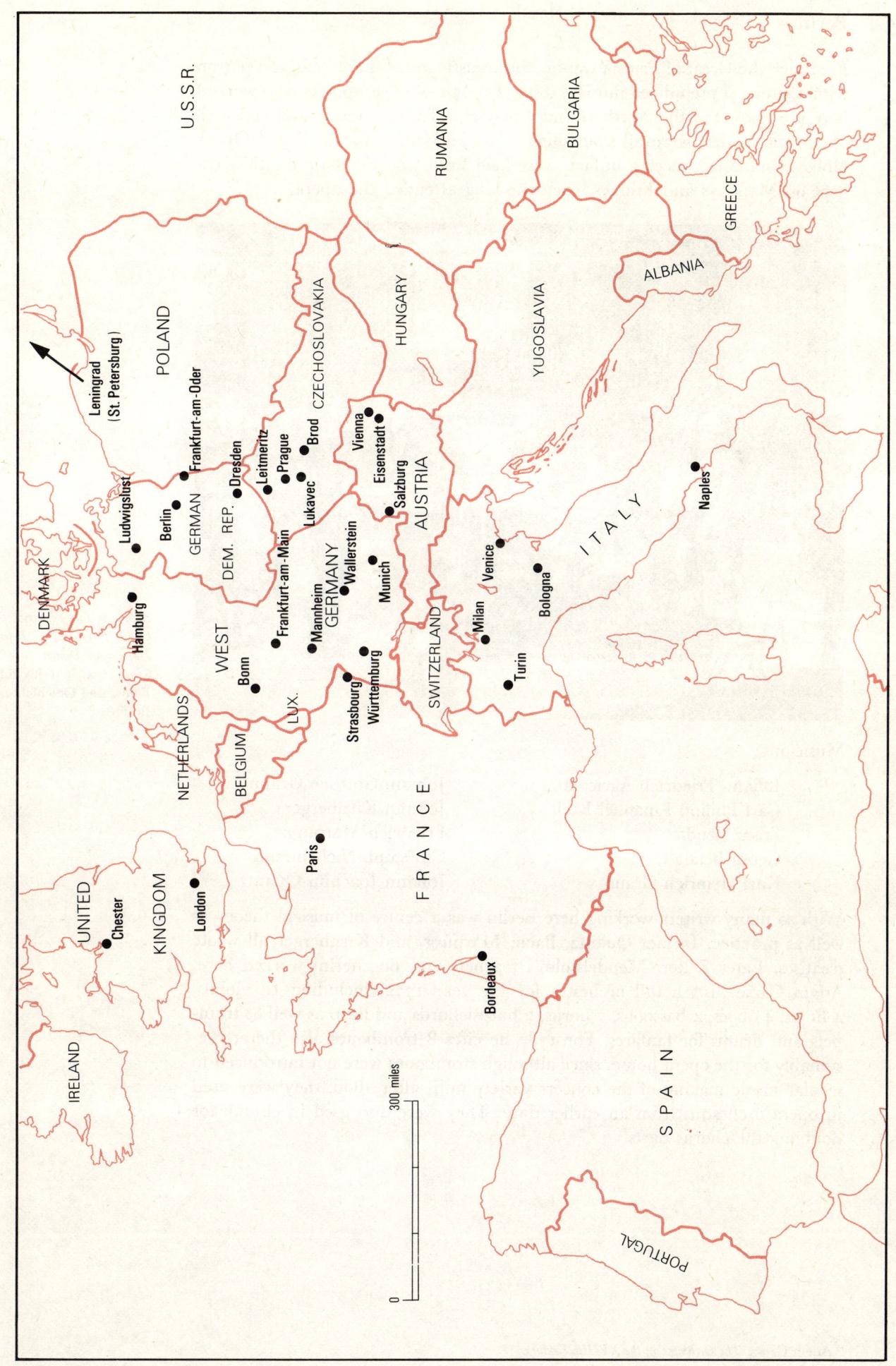

3.2 Berlin

Frederick the Great of Prussia was an enthusiastic musical amateur and patron with a strong if prejudiced musical taste. The school of composers who worked here are known as the North German School. Chamber music and concerts, opera and ballet, were all flourishing here and there was a Royal Opera House. Chamber concerts, in fact, were held from 7.00 to 9.00 p.m. daily except on Mondays and Fridays when the king attended the opera.

A concert with Frederick the Great. Engraving by Peter Hass, after Daniel Chodowiecki. (Archiv für Kunst und Geschichte, Berlin)

Musicians

Johann Friedrich Agricola
Carl Philipp Emanuel Bach
Franz Benda
Georg Benda
Karl Heinrich Graun

Johann Gottlieb Graun
Johann Kirnberger
Friedrich Marpurg
Christoph Nichelmann
Johann Joachim Quantz

With so many writers working here Berlin was a centre of musical theory as well as practice. In fact Quantz, Bach, Marpurg, and Kirnberger all wrote treatises. Later Zelter, Mendelssohn's teacher, and Boccherini worked here. Adam Carse[1] lists a full orchestra for the year 1772, including 12 violins, 4 flutes, 4 oboes, 4 bassoons, 2 horns, 2 harpsichords and harp as well as trumpets and drums for fanfares. For 1787 he cites 8 trombones also there, presumably for the opera house, since although trombones were not introduced to secular music making of the concert variety until after 1800, they were used in opera orchestras from an earlier date. They were also used in church for doubling the chorus parts.

[1] Adam Carse, *The Orchestra in the XVIIIth Century*.

Bologna

Here the patronage was civic or church, and the city itself had a long tradition of practical and theoretical study. The city university had a chair of music dating from 1450. There were three opera houses, the Teatro Matrezzi, which was destroyed by fire in 1745, Teatro Comunale, which opened in 1763 with an opera by Gluck, and the Teatro Marsigli Rossi. Of the many chapels, the most important were San Francesco and San Peronio. There were also three flourishing academies, whose aim was to patronize and direct the study of music. They gave diplomas which were highly coveted and difficult to win. The Accademia dei Floridi was founded in 1615, the Accademia dei Filaschisi in 1633, and, best known, the Accademia Filharmonica in 1666.

Musicians

G. B. Martini, known as Padre Martini, was the most influential teacher of his time, and was considered the greatest authority on theory, and his pupils included Jommelli, J. C. Bach, Gluck, Mozart and Grétry.

London

Italian opera was very popular in London and there were many theatres, notably the Queen's (or later the King's) Theatre at the Haymarket, Covent Garden Theatre, and Lincoln's Inn Theatre (where John Gay's *Beggar's Opera* was performed in 1728). There were countless societies, including Catch Clubs and Glee Clubs and a Philharmonic Society which sponsored weekly subscription concerts. Outdoor concerts were popular at Marylebone, Vauxhall and Ranelagh Gardens.

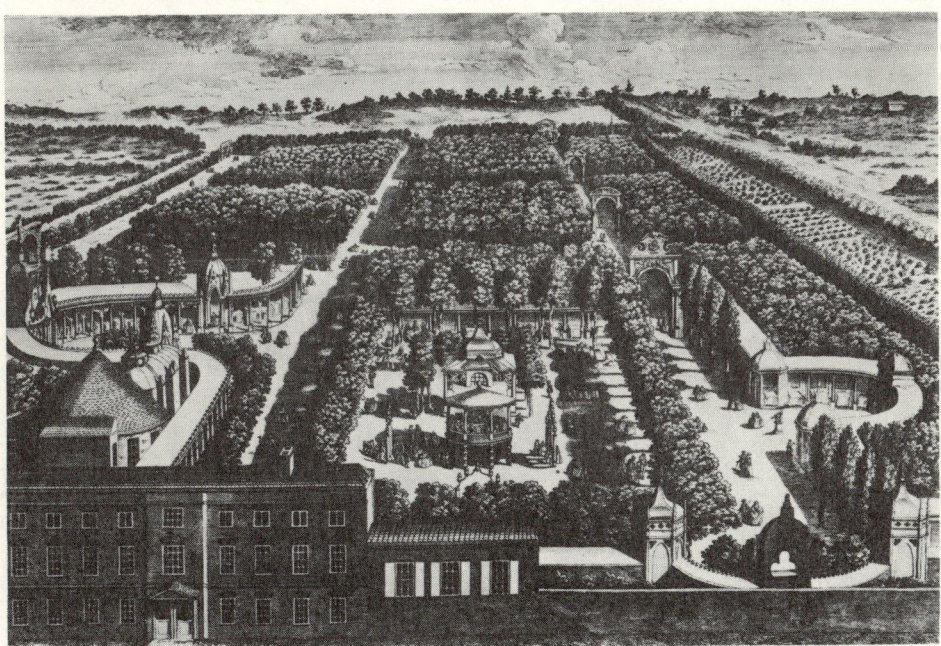

A general prospect of Vauxhall gardens. Designed by Wale, engraved by Muller (Mansell Collection)

Inside the Rotunda, Vauxhall, in 1752. Engraving by H. Robert (Mansell Collection)

Musicians

    Carl Friedrich Abel   [Baldassare Galuppi]
    Thomas Arne   [Christoph Willibald von Gluck]
    Johann Christian Bach   Maurice Greene
    William Boyce   [Franz Joseph Haydn]
    [Wilhelm Cramer]   Thomas Kelly
    [Johann Cramer]   [Wolfgang Amadeus Mozart]
    [Ernst Eichner]   John Christopher Pepusch

Carse lists a full orchestra in 1791 for the London Salomon Concerts, and this is quoted in the next block of units in this course, along with details of many other establishments.

Mannheim

The group of musicians that made the Mannheim School so important was employed by the Elector Palatine, Duke Carl Theodor. There was a chapel at Mannheim and a magnificent Knights' Hall for concerts, and an opera house at the summer palace outside Mannheim at Schwetzingen.

Musicians

        Johann Stamitz   Anton Filtz
                with   Ignaz Holzbauer
                                  Franz Xaver Richter

                and

    Franz Beck   Ignaz Fränzl
    Christian Cannabich   Johann Schobert
    Wilhelm Cramer   Anton Stamitz
    Johann Cramer   Karl Stamitz
    Franz Danzi   Alessandro Toeschi
    Ernst Eichner   Carlo Giuseppe Toeschi
    [Johann Christian Bach]
    [Georg Benda]   [Earl of Kelly]
    [Wolfgang Amadeus Mozart]

Carl Theodor, statue in Rittershall, Mannheim Castle (Landesbildstelle Baden)

The orchestra at Mannheim was renowned. In a letter to his father (of November 4th, 1777) Mozart tells him 'The orchestra is excellent and very strong' and consisted of 20 to 22 violins, 4 violas, 4 cellos, 4 double basses, double woodwind including clarinets and 4 bassoons, 2 horns, with trumpets and drums available.

Milan

A theatre for opera had been opened in the ducal palace in the early seventeenth century. This was destroyed by fire in 1776 and replaced two years later by the Teatro alla Scala, which opened with Salieri's *L'Europa riconosciuta* (Europe Rediscovered). Music flourished also at the cathedral, and private concerts in the homes of the nobility, and outdoor concerts in the grounds of Sforza Castle. The conservatoire, however, did not open until the early nineteenth century.

Musicians

Giovanni Battista Sammartini   [Johann Christian Bach]
                                      [Christoph Willibald von Gluck]
                                      [Wolfgang Amadeus Mozart]

The orchestra at Milan was judged to be the equal of Mannheim. At this time the taste was for instrumental music, oratorios and cantatas.

Paris

In between 1660 and 1800 there were successively about twenty-two theatres or establishments for the production of musical entertainment in Paris. Perhaps the best-known patron of the mid-eighteenth century was Alexandre-Jean-Joseph le Riche de la Pouplinière, who maintained a salon in Paris which Voltaire, Rousseau, Casanova and La Tour visited. Rameau was his organist, composer-in-residence and conductor. Paris was an important publishing centre.

Musicians

[Johann Christian Bach]	Ignaz Joseph Pleyel
[Georg Benda]	Nicola Piccini
[Christian Cannabich]	Jean Philippe Rameau
[Christoph Willibald von Gluck]	[Franz Anton Rosetti]
François Joseph Gossec	Jean Jacques Rousseau
[Wolfgang Amadeus Mozart]	[Johann Stamitz]

Paris appears to have been fairly cosmopolitan, although there was a native school of chamber music composers, and French string playing became increasingly important in Europe in the late eighteenth century, leading to the excellence of the Paris Conservatoire orchestra in the nineteenth century.

Vienna

Under Joseph I (1705–11) the Court Chapel (that is, musicians employed for court music-making connected with the chapel) increased to 107 members and he established two theatres, one for comic, one for serious opera. By the time of Maria Theresa (1740–80) instrumental music had become more popular. You will learn a lot more about Viennese music-making in the next section of the course.

Musicians

Carl Ditters von Dittersdorf	[Georg Benda]
Georg Matthias Monn	Christoph Williband von Gluck
Ignaz Joseph Pleyel	Franz Joseph Haydn
Georg Christoph Wagenseil	Wolfgang Amadeus Mozart
Johann Baptist Wanhal	[Niccolo Jommelli]

Vienna, of course, was to become the home of Classical instrumental music, and there appear to have been full orchestras at the opera and court in the early 1780s.

Exercise

Can you estimate the possible effect and influence of the mobility of composers?

Discussion

The free movement of composers throughout Europe led to quick dissemination of new music, styles, taste, ideas and developments. Reputations travelled equally fast and techniques of performance were criticised and admired or imitated. Composers were able to direct their own works in the way they wanted at different centres, and were thus able to establish some sort of authoritative standard, although eighteenth-century re-creations had different priorities from ours, and it is unlikely that contemporary performers were preoccupied with slavishly portraying the composer's intentions.

3.3 As you can see, although a great deal of patronage was in the hands of the aristocracy or church, opportunities for public participation and enjoyment in music were increasing. One most important development at this time, and certainly one that had considerable influence on the growth and popularity of the symphony, was that of the public and subscription concerts. In England, not only London but many smaller cities also established them. As Dr Stanley Sadie says in his Royal Musical Association paper 'Concert Life in Eighteenth-century England':

> Concert life in eighteenth-century England as a whole had a variety and vitality to which it would be hard to find a parallel. Not only were concerts held in the fashionable London salons, but in the 'Great Rooms' of taverns in villages which today are barely large enough to find a place on the map.

He goes on to discuss the enormous quantity and variety of concert promotions during the century up and down the country, pointing out that there was no such thing as a solo recital in the eighteenth century. All concerts were orchestral concerts, although often one or two solo singers were added. Outside London concerts were predominantly amateur, and the musical life at provincial cities, especially at cathedral cities which already had a nucleus of singers and possibly instrumentalists, was very active. In Norwich, especially, musical life was extremely flourishing. After 1714, according to a bye-law, the city waits had to give a monthly concert. There was also a weekly musical meeting in the early 1720s, and in 1736 yet another music club advertised that 'all lovers of Musick will meet with good wine and a hearty welcome'. By 1770 there were two regular subscription series and summer concerts in the pleasure gardens. Strange as it may seem to us, one traditional time for musical celebration was Assizes Week, and at Norwich public breakfasts and concerts were held in the open-air at this time.

Many other cities and towns had enterprising and flourishing musical lives: places such as York, Lincoln, Lichfield, Hereford, Oxford, Cambridge, Manchester, Birmingham, Leicester, Leeds, Wakefield, Halifax and Newcastle (whose relative sizes were less contrasted than they are today).

Benefit concerts (at which composers themselves or often their widows benefited from the proceeds) were especially useful in introducing new works to the public. Travelling musicians toured in troupes with concertos and other concert items. When Dr Arne passed through Shrewsbury returning from an Irish tour, the repertoire of his company included his own masques (*Comus* and *Alfred*), his own operas (*Rosamond* and *T. Thumb the Great*), Handel operas, *The Beggar's Opera* (by John Gay), concertos for violin, oboe and French horn and

> comic interludes after the Italian manner intended to give relief to that grave Attention, necessary to be kept up in serious Performances.[1]

---

[1] Quoted in Ernest Walker's *History of Music in England* (1952). p. 249.

3.4 It is possible to get some insight into the musical taste of the time by examining the catalogues of the music publishers. Music publishing had become enormously popular and successful. Cities like Paris and London had about sixteen firms each, whilst Amsterdam and Vienna had several, and Leipzig, Mannheim and Venice also had flourishing enterprises. Let us take London for example. In Burney's time in the 1760s the most successful music publisher was Bremner. His catalogue is divided up into the following categories, and gives us a good idea of the popularity of different sorts of music.

1. For concerts [i.e. orchestral music]
2. Periodical Overtures [i.e. so-called because they were printed in sets by publishers and issued periodically]
3. Italian Operas
4. Trios for 2 Violins and Bass
5. Duets for 2 Violins
6. Solos for a Violin and Bass
7. Solos for the German Flute and Bass [transverse flute]
8. Duets for 2 German Flutes
9. Trios for 2 German Flutes and a Bass
10. For the Harpsichord
11. For the Guitar
12. Vocal English
13. Vocal Italian
14. Scots Music
15. Miscellaneous
16. Treatises on Music

Among the music here the Scottish Earl of Kelly appears to have been both popular and successful. The Earl's teacher, 'The Elder Stamitz', is also represented, also Martini of Milan (i.e. Sammartini). Pugnani, Corelli, Alberti, Geminiani, Jommelli, Tessarini and many other well-known contemporary names. In *The Great Dr Burney*, Percy Scholes sums up what this list tells us as follows:

(a) Italian opera was a dominating style but English opera was beginning to make headway against it again, as it previously did from 1728 (i.e. from the appearance of *The Beggar's Opera*)[1] onward.

(b) Orchestral performance was developing and a good deal of provision was being made for it.

(c) In Chamber Music the viola had not yet come into its own and the popular style was the 'Trio for two Violins and Bass' (i.e. for two violins plus a figured bass for the harpsichord player, of which the actual bass line would be doubled by the violon-cellist).

(d) There was a considerable demand for Harpsichord Music, and the 'German Flute' and Guitar were also greatly favoured by amateurs.

(e) 'Garden Songs' (Vauxhall, etc.) were very popular, and simple Choral Music (e.g. *The Harmonists' Magazine* in monthly numbers) had a vogue.

(f) 'Scots Music' (folk-songs and quasi folk-songs in vocal form and instrumental arrangement and dance music) was a saleable commodity.

(g) Except for Handel oratorios (provided in another publisher's catalogue), the older contrapuntal style was dropping out of popularity and the newer (modern Sonata-form) style was beginning to come forward—as represented by Stamitz, J. C. Bach, the young Mozart, etc.

---

[1] *The Beggar's Opera* was the first English ballad opera and a rival to the successful Italian operas in London.

(h) Taking the nationality of composers in order of popularity we get first Italian, then German, then English—with the French (so active in their own country) practically unrepresented.

The concert societies and clubs were constantly demanding music, and new music too. Patronage of music was here swinging from the aristocracy and the church to the cultured middle classes, who made up the music-lovers and audiences. In London many societies for the promotion of music were flourishing. The Academy of Ancient Music for the study and practice of vocal and intrumental music was established in 1710 and flourished until 1792, meeting for a long time at the Crown and Anchor Tavern in the Strand under Pepusch, the German-born composer and impresario, theorist and teacher. Choristers from St Paul's Cathedral and the Chapel Royal were engaged to sing at concerts. The music making in the London pleasure gardens such as Ranelagh, Marylebone and Vauxhall was very popular. The musicians were made up of instrumentalists and vocalists free and looking for work at the end of the opera season, which ran from October to March. Composers represented at these summer concerts included Handel, Mozart, J. C. Bach, Stanley, Charles Avison, William Boyce, Charles Burney, Arne, Dibdin, Thomas Linley (the elder) and James Hook. Mozart played at Ranelagh gardens. As his father wrote to a friend Lorenz Hagenauer in Salzburg,

The Ranelagh Orchestra. Detail from 'The Ranelagh Rotunda' by Canaletto (National Gallery)

> On Friday, June 29th [1764], that is, on the feast of St Peter and St Paul, there will be a concert or benefit at Ranelagh in aid of a newly established *Hôspital de Femmes en couche*, and whoever wishes to attend it must pay five shillings entrance. I am letting Wolfgang play a concerto on the organ at this concert in order to perform thereby the act of an English patriot who, as far as in him lies, endeavours to further the usefulness of this hospital which has been established *pro bono publico*.

The subscription concerts founded by J. C. Bach and C. F. Abel in the same year were at Carlisle House, Soho Square till 1775 and then at the new Hanover Square Rooms. Talking of subscription concerts, Burney says:

> Another was established by Mrs Corneley, in Soho-Square, where the best performers and the best company were assembled, till Bach and Abel, uniting interests, opened a new subscription, about 1763, for a weekly concert, and as their own compositions were new and excellent, and the best performers of all kinds which our capital could supply enlisted under their banners, this concert was better patronized and longer supported than perhaps any one had ever been in this country; having continued for full twenty years with uninterrupted prosperity.

3.5 Whatever musical centre you might be interested in Burney has probably visited it, and there are fascinating first-hand details of the musical life all over Europe in the volumes written by him about his travels in Germany, Italy and France. There are also splendid and scholarly accounts of music in the Duchy of Parma, and at the courts of Charles Eugène of Württembêrg, Maria Antonia of Saxony and Frederick the Great of Prussia in *Music at Court: Four Eighteenth Century Studies* by Alan Yorke-Long.

However, the musical centre which, besides being most interesting, is the most important to us in the present study, is the court at Mannheim. Between 1742 and 1778 Duke Carl Theodor, Elector Palatine,[1] held court at Mannheim.

In 1778, the year after he inherited the throne of the Bavarian Wittelsbach family, he transferred his court and most of the musicians to Munich. It is the Elector's court orchestra at Mannheim that became so renowned and admired throughout Europe. The term 'Mannheim school' refers to the style of virtuoso and ensemble playing, and symphonic writing, that became such a tradition there. The founder was violinist and musical director Johann Stamitz, whom Carl Theodor had heard and tempted to Mannheim in 1742. Stamitz's pupil and successor Cannabich made the standard of playing even more virtuosic and professional. Mozart, visiting in 1778, thought Cannabich the best conductor he had ever seen, and Dr Burney was quite overwhelmed.

When he visited there he found the city and court one entity. In 1720 the Prince Elector Karl Philipp had removed his residence from Heidelberg to Mannheim, and planned there a palace that would compete with Versailles. A hunting lodge and summer palace in Schwetzingen with immense parks were situated nearby. In Mannheim itself there was a palace, a Jesuit chapel, an observatory, Old City Hall and arsenal, and at Schwetzingen gardens, alleys and grand fountains designed to ornament his spacious summer palace, and a theatre.

---

[1] The Elector Palatine was the ruler of the Rhineland and one of the electors of the Holy Roman Emperor.

A304 Units 12–13

Mannheim Castle
(Landesbildstelle Baden)

Staircase, Mannheim Castle
(Landesbildstelle Baden)

Old Town Hall, Mannheim
(Reissmuseum Mannheim;
Photo Landesdenkmalamt
Baden-Württemberg)

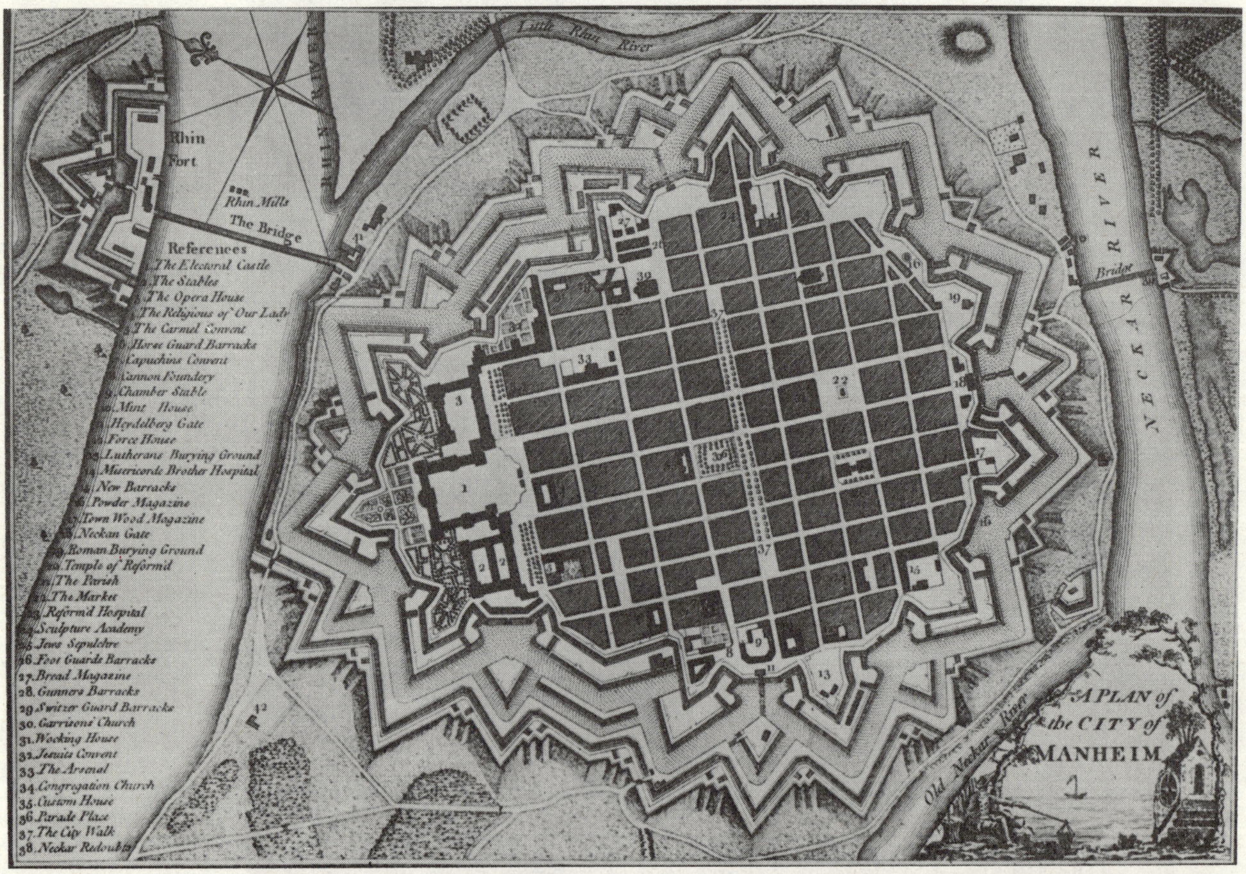

Plan of Mannheim c 1800 (Radio Times Hulton Picture Library)

Jesuit Church, Mannheim
(Landesdenkmalamt
Baden-Württemberg)

Arsenal, Mannheim (Landesbildstelle Baden)

The city itself was created at the drawing board. It was designed forming an oblong circle and is divided up into eleven longitudinal and ten transverse streets of appropriate width and cut into 112 blocks.

The palace is now a university and the Knights' Hall, where all the original instrumental concerts took place, is still in use (and for the same purpose too).

Knights' Hall, Mannheim Castle (Landesbildstelle Baden)

When Dr Burney paid his visit in 1772 the Court was in its summer resort of Schwetzingen. He attended the performance of a comic opera by Sacchini at the Elector's Theatre and was more than enthusiastic about the music. Under Stamitz, who had been musical director until his death in 1757,

> every effect had been tried, which such an aggregate of sound could produce.

Theatre interior, Schwetzingen (Burgermeisteramt der Stadt Schwetzingen)

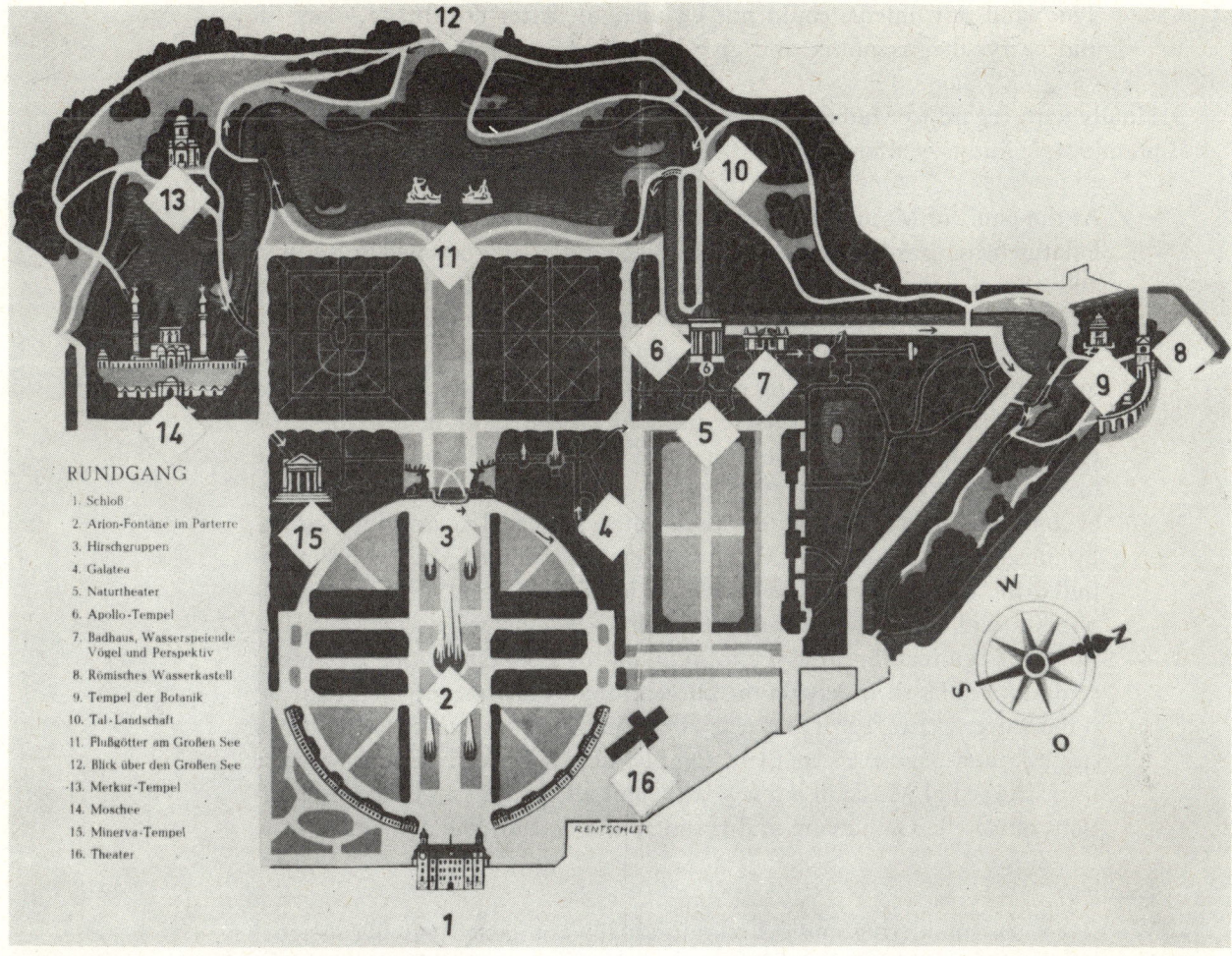

Fig. 14. Plan of Schwetzingen (Landesbildstelle Baden)

Key:
1. Castle
2. Fountains and ornamental gardens
3. Deer group statues
4. Galatea
5. Outdoor theatre
6. Temple of Apollo
7. Spa, watergardens, aviary and avenues
8. 'Roman' moated castle
9. Temple of Botany
10. Arbour
11. River gods and large lake
12. Viewpoint over large lake
13. Temple of Mercury
14. Mosque
15. Temple of Minerva
16. Theatre

(Nevertheless, Dr Burney had some criticism of 'the want of truth [tuning] in the wind instruments'.)

The establishment at Mannheim was extremely conducive to the developments of the arts. The Elector himself played the flute and cello and gave concerts, which were free to everyone, on nights when there was no opera. Of his 1,500 employees, a good proportion were musicians.

> To a stranger walking through the streets of Schwetzingen, during the summer, this place must seem to be inhabited only by a colony of musicians, who are constantly expressing their profession: at one house a fine player on the violin is heard; at another, a German flute; here an excellent hautbois; there a bassoon, a clarinet, a violoncello, or a concert of several instruments together. Music seems to be the chief and most constant of his electoral highness's amusements: and the operas, and concerts, to which all his subjects have admission, form the judgement, and establish a taste for music, throughout the electorate.

Schubart[1] in his *Essays on Musical Esthetics* (1806) says of the Mannheim music:

> One believed oneself to be transported to a magic island of sound.... No orchestra in the world ever equalled the Mannheimer execution. Its forte is like thunder; its crescendo like a mighty water-fall; its diminuendo a gentle river disappearing into the distance; its piano is a breath of spring.

---

[1] Christian Schubart, 1739–91, German author, organist and composer who lived at Mannheim for a while.

> The wind instruments could not be used to better advantage; they lift
> and carry, they reinforce and give life to the storm of the violins.

Finally with regard to Mannheim Burney sums up the impact of the new symphonic style and execution:

> At the court of Mannheim, about the year 1759, the band of the Elector Palatine was regarded as the most complete and best disciplined in Europe; and the symphonies that were produced by the maestro di capella, Holtzbaur,[1] the elder Stamitz, Filz, Cannabich, Toeski and Fräntzel, became the favourite full-pieces of every concert, and supplanted concertos and opera overtures, being more spirited than the one, and more solid than the other. Though these symphonies seemed at first to be little more than an improvement of the opera overtures of Jomelli, yet, by the fire and genius of Stamitz (1717–57) they were exalted into a new species of composition, at which there was an outcry, as usual against innovation, by those who wish to keep Music stationary. The late Mr Avison[2] attributed the corruption and decay of Music to the torrent of modern symphonies with which we were over-whelmed from foreign countries. But though I can readily subscribe to many of the opinions of that ingenious writer, we differ so widely on this subject, that it has long seemed to me as if the variety, taste, spirit and new effects produced by contrast and use of *crescendo* and *diminuendo* in these symphonies, had been of more service to instrumental Music in a few years, than all the dull and servile imitations of Corelli, Geminiani, and Handel, had been in half a century.

Exercise

We have been considering musical establishments and concert-giving societies and patrons. You will have realized that musical patronage can be divided into three main categories. Can you suggest the three groups of musicians?

Discussion

The three main categories are (i) Court musicians, (ii) church musicians, (iii) opera and theatre musicians.

(i) There were musicians attached to court (and according to J. N. Forkel, the German music historian of the late eighteenth and early nineteenth century, there were more than 340 courts in German-speaking Europe alone in 1754). They were permanently engaged as part of the household, and their status within it depended on circumstances and seniority. The patronage here was of an absolute kind. However, this in itself gave a certain amount of artistic freedom. There were obvious advantages in working in this sort of residential establishment: security for one, the opportunities for the formation of a constant ensemble and tradition; the opportunities for experimentation; and the financial backing.

(ii) Musicians involved in or employed by the church. These were of course mainly vocalists or organist/choir trainer/composers, although in a situation like J. S. Bach's in Leipzig, he had the means to employ orchestral players, and

---

[1] Burney's spelling varies from present-day practice.
[2] Charles Avison (*c.* 1710–70), English composer.

to rehearse and perform his bigger works like the cantatas and Passions with them. On his appointment in 1723 he signed an undertaking of his duties, which contained fourteen clauses describing them, and ending:[1]

> Now therefore I do hereby undertake and bind myself faithfully to observe all of the said requirements, and on pain of losing my post not to act contrary to them, in witness whereof I have set my hand and seal to this agreement.
>
> Done in Leipzig, May 5th, 1723.

(iii) The third big category is of musicians employed by opera houses and theatres. Singers, instrumentalists and composers were hired on a seasonal basis, leaving them free during the summer months to seek concert work on a free-lance basis. Benedetto Marcello gives some interesting information on theatre musicians in his satirical book of 1721 *Il teatro alla modo* (Theatre à la mode) which gives a witty and at times caustic account of the abuse that the opera world had fallen into at that time. Subtitled *A sure and easy method to compose well and to produce Italian operas in the modern fashion*, it sets out to give advice to all the people concerned. The would-be librettist is informed that no familiarity with the classics is necessary, in fact he should give no thought to literary style or poetic metre, but compose verse by verse without preconceived plan, borrowing wherever possible from other authors, even translating from the French. Length of arias and construction of scenes must depend upon the sets, décors, bears, lions, earthquakes and lightning machines and other apparatus available. 'The disintegration of the drama as an entity and the intense boredom of the audience are of no importance in connection with all this.' The composer is likewise instructed that he is best equipped without any technical skill or knowledge whatsoever. Perhaps most revealing of all is the advice: 'Noise is what counts in modern music, not harmonious sound.' From a closer study of the work we could derive a fair indication of the general atmosphere and conditions under which Italian theatre musicians lived and worked in the early part of the century.

3.7 There were all sorts of other musicians in more independent situations, like Handel and J. C. Bach in London, who ran their own businesses in a most professional manner. However, it seems to have been the ambition among many musicians to acquire security in the employ of one of the better permanent establishments. Mozart tried hard to get some sort of position at the Mannheim court, and remained there many months in the hope of it, sending his father details of his progress:

> Mannheim, 10 December 1777
>
> Mon très cher Père!
>
> There's nothing to be hoped for at present [from the Elector]. The day before yesterday I went to the concert at Court to get his [answer. Count Savioli] studiously avoided me, but I made my way up to him. When he saw me, he shrugged his shoulders. 'What', I said, 'No answer yet?' 'Please forgive me', he replied, 'Unfortunately none.' 'Eh bien', I said, 'the Elector might have told me so before.' 'True', he said, 'but he would not have made up his mind even now, if I had not prodded him and pointed out that you had been hanging on here for such a long time and were using up all your money at the inn.' 'That's what worries me most of all', I retorted. 'It's not at all nice. However, I am very much obliged

---

[1] Quoted in *The Bach Reader* by David and Mendel, p. 92.

to you, Count (we don't address him as Your Excellency), for having taken such an interest in me, and I beg you to thank [the Elector] on my behalf for his gracious though belated reply, and to say that I can assure him that he would never have regretted it if he had taken me on.'

(The brackets indicate a translation of the code Mozart used when he wanted to avoid mentioning names.)

4.0 EDUCATION

4.1 The opportunities for musical education in different European countries varied considerably. Italy was unique in possessing conservatoires at Naples and Venice providing professional musical education from the age of eight to eighteen. Such establishments produced a considerable number of fine executant musicians and composers. Pergolesi, the Neapolitan opera composer, was educated at the Conservatorio Dei Poveri di Gesù Cristo (Conservatoire of the Poor of Jesus Christ) in Naples and had his first major work, an oratorio, commissioned when still a senior student there. When Dr Burney visited Naples in 1770 the scholars in the conservatoires had the reputation, so he said, of being the foremost contrapuntists and composers in Europe. In a conversation with Piccini,[1] he inquired after these institutions and learned that there were three in Naples with altogether over four hundred scholars. Each had two principal *maestri di capella* or directors, one to superintend composition and the other singing, and there were assistant masters, called *maestri secolari*, one for each instrument. The boys were admitted at the age of eight or ten and stayed until they were about twenty. The general noisiness that distressed Dr Burney so in the theatre is in accord with what he found when he visited the Conservatoire of S. Onofrio. He writes:

> In a common practice room there was a 'Dutch Concert'—consisting of seven or eight harpsichords, more than as many violins, and several voices all performing different things in different keys. The violoncellos practise in another room; and the flutes, hautbois and other wind instruments, in a third, except the trumpets and horns which are obliged to play either on the stairs or in the top of the house.

During the winter the boys rose two hours before light, and worked until eight o'clock in the evening, with a break of an hour and a half at dinner. This constant perseverence for a number of years, with genius and good teaching, Dr Burney considered, must have produced great musicians.

The three conservatoires in Naples were for boys. Those in Venice were for girls: Dr Burney describes them as:

> Female orphanages where the children, so far as their natural capabilities allowed, were brought up to music, being taught to sing and to play the various stringed and wind instruments by the best masters in Italy.

Some of the singing moved Burney to tears: these girls, he said, had 'a facility of executing difficult compositions equal to that of birds', and did 'such things in that way as he did not remember to have heard attempted before'.

---

[1] The Naples-born opera composer who achieved such notoriety in Paris as a rival to Gluck.

4.2 However, these institutions were unique and elsewhere, after perhaps an excellent musical start as a chorister (like Haydn or Burney) it was a matter of private lessons or musical apprenticeship for those wishing to become professional musicians. For those who wished to be educated musically without a career in mind, there were private lessons from established masters.

4.3 If we look at the musical education of a couple of well-known eighteenth-century figures we can see the sort of opportunities that were available. Charles Burney helped himself to a fine musical education, and J. C. Bach, youngest son of J. S. Bach, was also widely experienced.

Charles Burney, English composer and writer, to whom anyone interested in the music of the period continually refers, was the son of James MacBurney, and was educated first at the Free Grammar School in Shrewsbury, then, when his family moved, at the Public School, now the King's School, in Chester. In Shrewsbury he served as a chorister and learnt the organ and harpsichord with the parson. He became pupil and assistant to Edmund Baker, organist of Chester Cathedral, and was taught to play 'chants enough to keep the organ going'. Later he had lessons from Mr Orme,[1] the next organist, who also had 'a great collection of music by the best Italian composers of the time', to which Burney had access, and which no doubt was eagerly devoured by him.

At sixteen Burney returned to Shrewsbury to become pupil and assistant to his half-brother James MacBurney.[2]

> The celebrated Felton,[3] and after him the first Dr Hayes, came from Oxford to Shrewsbury on a tour, while I was studying hard, without instruction or example; and they amazed and stimulated me so forcibly by their performance on the organ, as well as by their encouragement, that I thence-forward went to work with an ambition and fury that would hardly allow me to eat or sleep.
>
> The quantity of music which I copied at this time, of all kinds, was prodigious; and my activity and industry surprised everybody, for, besides writing, teaching, tuning and playing for my brother, at my *moments perdus*, I was educating myself in every way I was able with copy books. I improved my hand-writing so much, that my father did not believe I wrote my letters to him myself. I tried hard to at least keep up the little Latin I had learned; and I diligently practised both the spinet and the violin; which with reading, transcribing music for business, and poetry for pleasure; attempts at composition, and attention to my brother's affairs, filled up every minute of the longest day.
>
> I had also, a great passion for angling; but whenever I could get leisure to pursue this sport, I ran no risk of losing any time, if the fish did not bite; for I had always a book in my pocket which enabled me to wait with patience their pleasure.

In 1744, back in Chester with his father, he continued to study hard. About this time Dr Arne was passing through Chester from Dublin to London, with his troupe of musicians, on a concert-giving tour. Impressed by young Burney, he made:

> an offer to Mr Burney, senior, *upon such conditions as are usual to such short*

---

[1] Edward Orme (1764–76), organist.

[2] James MacBurney or Burney (1705–89).

[3] William Felton (1715–69), clergyman, organist, harpsichordist and composer.

of patronage [my italics] to complete the education of this lively and aspiring young man, and to bring him forth as his favourite and most promising pupil.

The year after Burney's arrival with Dr Arne in London, Arne was appointed both leader at Drury Lane and composer to Vauxhall Gardens. He also was kept fully occupied with commissions from Ranelagh and Marylebone and young Burney was busily and profitably employed copying, orchestrating, arranging, coaching singers and filling in on the harpsichord or whatever string instrument was in short supply. In fact Burney complained that Arne gave him very little instruction, but he must have had invaluable experience.

Dr. Arne composing 'Rule Britannia'. Adapted from an engraving by Richard Bentley (Mansell Collection)

Of course, Dr Burney's education never finished—he was educating himself for the rest of his life. During his famous and well-documented European tours he lost no opportunity to meet and talk with eminent teachers and musicians, and hear music of every sort. He must have been one of the most knowledgeable musicians of his age.

Johann Christian Bach, on the other hand, came from a long tradition of eminent professional musicians. At fifteen, on his father's death (he was the youngest of a large family) he was taken into the household of his elder half-brother (Carl Philipp Emanuel Bach, already a successful versatile musician), who continued to teach him composition and performance. In Berlin, where C. P. E. Bach then lived and worked, Frederick the Great inaugurated frequent extravagant operatic productions. Admission was free, and thus J. C. Bach became familiar with Italian operas of the German composers like Hasse, Graun and Agricola that were performed there. In 1755 or 1756, at twenty years old, he left the family of his brother to study in Italy. Here as protégé of the Italian Count Litta of Milan, he assimilated Italian styles, playing in the private orchestra of his patron and continuing studies under the famous teacher Padre Giovanni Battista Martini of Bologna. He became a Catholic, a big step for someone with his background, and wrote church music. In 1760 he became organist of Milan Cathedral and at the same time continued his broad education, visiting Naples for the opera at the *Teatro di San Carlo* which was so famous for its 50-piece orchestra and world-renowned singers, and composing operas. He finally left Italy for England at the invitation of Colomba Mattei to become official composer to the King's Theatre for the season 1762–3, and after this London became his chief home.

4.4 Musical education was furthered, too, by the undoubted influence of touring virtuoso performers, such as Mozart, and the mobility of musicians themselves. Ordinary rank-and-file musicians obviously had limited freedom, but someone like J. C. Bach was born and initially educated in Leipzig, then Berlin, Milan, Bologna and finally London. From here he travelled to other centres such as Paris and Mannheim, taking his own music with him. He must have been well aware of contemporary local styles and developments. Dissemination of music was increasing with the boom in music publishing. We've already seen that Bremner's catalogues give an idea of the amount of music itself that was in demand. Charles Cudworth, in his paper 'The Vauxhall "Lists" ' (*The Galpin Society Journal* XX) gives a résumé of symphonic music performed at Vauxhall Gardens in the 1790 season, which ran from mid-May to the end of August. He lists the number of times a composer is mentioned, which in itself gives us some idea of the accessibility and popularity of their works. This is not the complete list, but here are some of the names with which you will probably be familiar.

Composer	*Times Mentioned*
Haydn	85
Pleyel	38
Handel	36
Bach (i.e. J. C.)	33
Stamitz (no initial)	21
Hook	16
Abel	13
Arne	9
Richter	7
Boyce	4
Fisher	4
Gossec	3
Toeschi	3
Jommelli	1
Philidor	1
Dittersdorf	1

By the way, from 1774 to 1820 James Hook (see above, six down) was resident organist at the Vauxhall Pleasure Gardens, where he was expected to play a concerto a night in the season—not all of his own composing, presumably!

4.5 If his work was published, the composer was obliged to try to safeguard it by including more explicit instructions, because it would travel beyond his personal supervision. And of course the new style was more expressive—at least it had a different kind of expressiveness perhaps, which required more detailed explanation. The composer wanted to dictate much more exactly how his music was to be performed and this led to the use of directions for tempo, expression, dynamics and so on, which were used much more consistently and systematically. Look at this extract of full score (marked up by the composer), for example, and notice how carefully Rosetti has thought out how he wants every note played.

5.0 PERFORMANCE PRACTICE

5.1 By 'performance practice' we mean the way in which music is performed. When we are talking about eighteenth-century music it refers to conventions in distribution of parts, manner of phrasing and bowing, realization of short-hands such as continuo parts and ornamentations, and other interpretative factors that would have been more familiar to contemporary musicians. I say 'more' familiar, because although certain performance practices were so well known that it was unnecessary to explain them, others even at the time had to be taught or explained. This is fortunate for us because it resulted in the publication of a number of treatises concerning musical interpretation that we find most useful today. Since they range from the specific to the general in their subjects and discuss questions of such importance as contemporary style, performance practice, and aesthetics, they are invaluable. Among the most important of these eighteenth-century treatises are:

1. J. J. Quantz: *Versuch einer Anweisung die Flöte transversière zu spielen* (1752) (Flute-playing method).[1]
2. Leopold Mozart: *Versuch einer gründlichen Violinschule* (1756) (Violin method).
3. C. P. E. Bach: *Versuch über die wahre Art, das Clavier zu spielen* (1753) (Essay on the true art of playing keyboard instruments).

Extracts from these three and from other relevant contemporary writings can be found translated in *Source Readings in Music History: The Classic Era*, selected and annotated by Oliver Strunk.[2]

5.3 Another valuable source of information is surviving performing parts themselves and we can presume a great deal about how composers felt about the way in which symphonic music was performed by a look at contemporary parts. Symphonies, overtures, concertos, suites and so on were sold separately in parts, and full scores of them were hardly ever published. Parts for optional instruments, or instruments that might not always have been available in every orchestra, were on sale separately, often in manuscript. The late Professor Thurston Dart in his book *The Interpretation of Music* quotes title pages containing remarks like:

> double-basses, trumpets and timpani will greatly add to the effect of this piece; those who require parts for them should get in touch with M. Lallemand, the copyist of the Opera House. (1750)

and

> Six symphonies in four parts, with optional parts for horns, by M. Stamitz. The horn parts are on sale separately. (1755)

This performance practice, and those of doubling violin parts on oboes, including bassoon whether stipulated or not, and adding a viola to double the bass line an octave higher, must apply only to the earlier part of our period, since by the time our later case studies were written the woodwind parts are really independent, and indiscriminate doubling would ruin the thought-out balance and textures. Horns and trumpets were doubtless interchangeable for some time, although it was not long before brass instruments became both individual and essential, requiring idiomatically written parts.

5.3 It seems that a keyboard continuo instrument was used in all symphonic works until the time that textures and orchestral refinements became too detailed and subtle to need it. Even when its original role, that of filling out the texture and harmony, was no longer needed, the definition given by a harpsichord was expected and its presence would have been missed from the total tonal sonority.

5.4 And that brings us on to the question of conducting. Although the idea of a conductor as interpreter obviously had its roots during these early years of the symphony's development, it was not until the nineteenth century that the art of conducting grew to importance, especially in Germany. During the middle of the eighteenth century it was customary to direct opera performances from the harpsichord. Instrumental music, however, was usually directed by the

---

[1] This essay, however, contains much more than its title implies, especially about musical performance practice.

[2] New York 1965. Paperback edition volume IV. *The Classic Era.*

first violin from his leader's place: Stamitz and Cannabich did this at Mannheim. When Haydn visited London in 1791 and 1794 control of the orchestra was shared between Haydn as a keyboard player at the harpsichord, and Salomon with his violin. (It is worth noting that even composers we think of as primarily keyboard executants learnt the violin as a matter of course—Bach, Handel, Mozart, Beethoven for example—and as often as not earned their first money as orchestral musicians. There was not the 'us and them' situation which tends to exist today between keyboard players and orchestral musicians.) The rise of the conductor as the dominating figure is undoubtedly linked to the rise of refinement and precision in performance that is connected with Mannheim and the Mannheim school.

6.0 **TECHNOLOGICAL DEVELOPMENT AND ORCHESTRATION**

6.1 There is no doubt that between the Handel/Bach type of orchestration of the first half of the eighteenth century, and the style of Haydn and Mozart, there was a complete change of thinking about the orchestra and its role. The new style of orchestration grew up gradually during the first half of the century, along with the change of music style and the gradually waning popularity of contrapuntally conceived music. This new style of orchestration was at first completely dependent on the new harmonic style of the post-Baroque composers.

6.2 It is possible to trace some sort of development in this change in orchestration in Italy through Alessandro Scarlatti and Jommelli, in France through Rameau and Gluck, and in Germany and Austria through Hasse, Wagenseil and Gluck (who worked in Vienna before his ten years at the Paris *Opéra* between 1770 and 1780).

6.3 The Baroque orchestra was variable and erratic. Since brass and woodwind instruments were used as melodic instruments and not for sustaining harmony, composers used those types of instruments that they had available indiscriminately. Here are a few bars of score from Bach's Suite no. 4 in D major for trumpets, drums, oboes, bassoon, strings and continuo:

Bach: Suite no. 4 in D Major

At the opening all the instruments join in the contrapuntal movement regardless of their suitability or the balance of parts. Were there voice parts they would be virtually indistinguishable from the instrumental parts.

An entirely new idea, and not one that could readily co-exist with contrapuntal style, was to use instruments to sustain harmony, accompany other melodic instruments, give a background of harmonic energy as strings could, or join forces to produce an entirely new sound, an orchestral tutti, as in this page of score from Stamitz' Symphony in G major op. 3 no. 1.

Sinfonia a 8

Johann Stamitz, Op. 3. N° 1.

6.4 The new stylistic concept of a tune and accompaniment provided opportunities for the invention of all sorts of variations in accompanying figures. Chords could be sustained or repeated, or broken into figurations or rhythmical patterns. They could have a variety of textures, such as pizzicato (plucked strings) or detached chords or sustained unmoving harmony. Timbre could now be considered for its own sake, and the effect of groups of instruments from the point of view of colour could be explored. The basso continuo began to be dropped and the specific direction 'senza cembalo' (without harpsichord) can be found in scores. Not only was the harmonic support no longer necessary, since the woodwind and horns and lower strings had filled out the harmonic gaps, but the consistent plucked-string tone-colour became foreign to the new orchestral sonority, and although a continuo instrument, usually the harpsichord, was still used in the orchestra until the late eighteenth century, some composers began specifically to exclude it (for example C. P. E. Bach in the slow movement of our case study symphony). Horns were used to blend in, to add colour, cohesion and volume, as in the opening of this symphony by J. C. Bach:

J. C. Bach: Symphony in E♭ major

Trumpets and drums are used to emphasize climaxes and to add excitement. The last seven bars of the first movement of the J. C. Bach case study shown opposite are an example of this technique.

Individual instruments were used as tone colours, material being passed from one to another. This in itself was quite a change from the Baroque custom of setting a tone colour at the beginning of a movement and continuing with it practically unchanged until the end. That is not to deny the variety it was possible to achieve within these limits, however. In his *The History of Orchestration* Adam Carse sums up the effect of this change in style. I summarize his conclusions below.

1 Flute parts tend to lie higher, and when they double oboe parts they do so in the octave above. Flute techniques such as embellishment [characteristic ornamentation] begin to feature.

2 Oboes and bassoon parts become less florid and more sustained. They are liable to be used together as harmony instruments. As the element of imitative counterpoint declines, the woodwind no longer necessarily echo string-passages and figures. They achieve individuality and are no longer so busily active as the flutes.

3 Horn parts are lower in pitch, and lose their conjunct melodic characteristics.

4 Trumpet parts become lower and more manageable and are used mainly with rhythmical patterns of characteristic design, marking accents, underlying rhythms and adding in general to the tutti.

5 String parts gain variety and freedom for effects such as pizzicato, tremolo, reiteration of the same note, figures based on the facility with which the bow can be made to alternate rapidly between two notes on adjacent strings and double-stopping.

Clarinets[1] became popular from the middle of the century onwards. At Mannheim they were used early in the works of K. Stamitz, Beck, Toeschi and Holzbauer. Elsewhere in Germany they became used more gradually. In Paris they were regular members of La Pouplinière's orchestra and a programme for a *concert spirituel* in 1755 listed a clarinet in a symphony by Johann Stamitz. Gossec and J. C. Bach also used them occasionally. But they were not established members of the orchestra until the end of the century.

6.5 You will have read about technological development in instruments of the string and woodwind families in previous units. You can read about technical development in the horn and the trumpet in your set book *Musical Instruments through the Ages* (pp. 295–300 and 286–91).

Until the eighteenth century the horn came in one piece, geared ideally for playing music in one key only because of its dependence on the notes produced by the player's use of lip-control or embouchure from the harmonic series. The fundamental pitch of the horn, and therefore all the related notes was dependent on the tube length. For any change of key it was necessary to use another horn with a different tube length and therefore a different consequent range of notes. In about 1715 a horn was produced in Vienna whose length could be altered at the mouthpiece end by terminal rings of tubing of assorted sizes called 'crooks'. The horn could be put into any required key by inserting the necessary crook. During the middle of the century, some Bohemian composers realized that although the upper register of the horn was reasonably possible (the 'conjunct melodic characteristics' mentioned by Carse) there were gaps in the middle compass that could be filled by altering the pitch of the note by the insertion of the hand in the bell. A Dresden horn player, A. J. Hampel, first made this practice well known and trained many pupils in it, although this 'stopping'[2] was little used by orchestral players as distinct from solo players. In about 1750 a new design of more manageable shape to give freer blowing was proposed by Hampel, which left the mouthpipe fixed while the crooks fitted into the body of the horn. This new design was known as an 'Inventions horn'. Terminal crooks, separate for each key, came back into use, however, towards the end of the century. With all these 'improvements' went considerable problems of controlling intonation.

We've already talked about the change in trumpet writing during the eighteenth century from the Baroque manner of Bach and Handel to the new manner of the early Classical composers. The trumpet's popularity as a solo instrument declined with the changing style of composition, partly because players lost their cultivated technique of sustained playing in a higher register, and

---

[1] Anthony Baines discusses the technical development of the clarinet in *Musical Instruments through the Ages* (pp. 244–247).

[2] 'Stopping' actually narrows the bore and therefore lowers the pitch of a note a semitone. If the hand is inserted suddenly in the bell, however, the pitch of the note is raised a semitone and acquires a muffled quality.

A304 Units 12–13

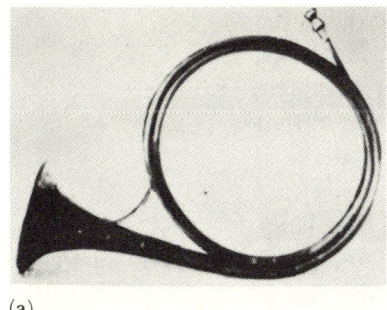
(a)

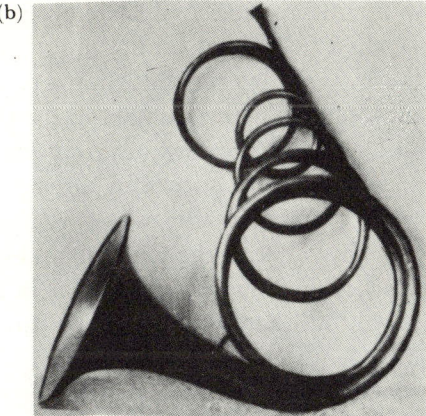
(b)

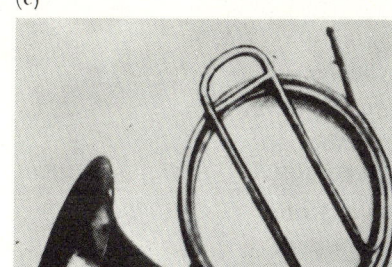
(c)

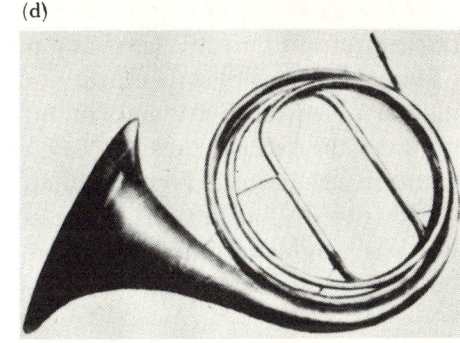
(d)

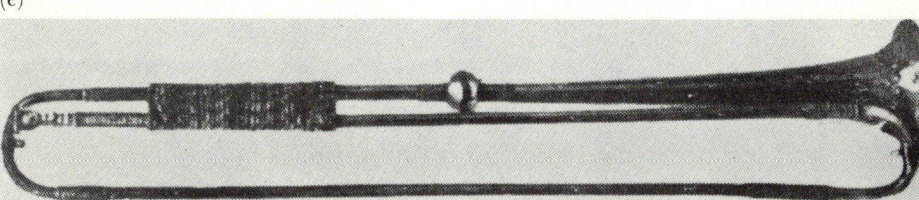
(e)

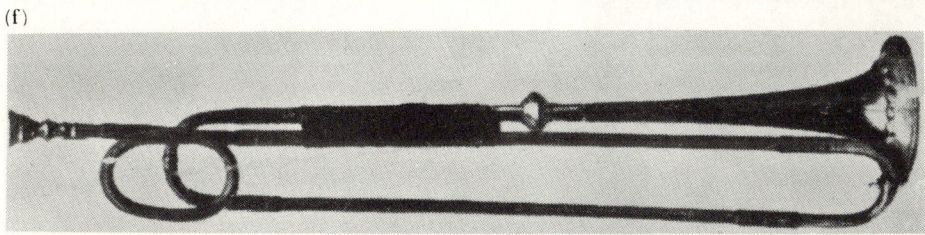
(f)

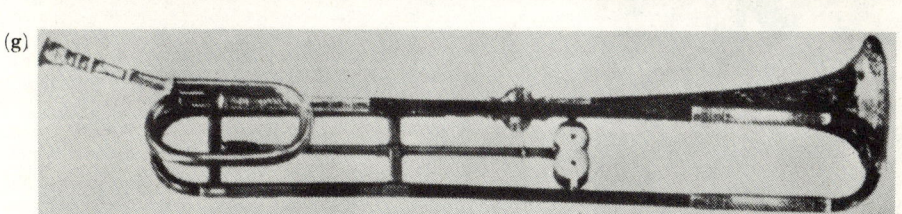
(g)

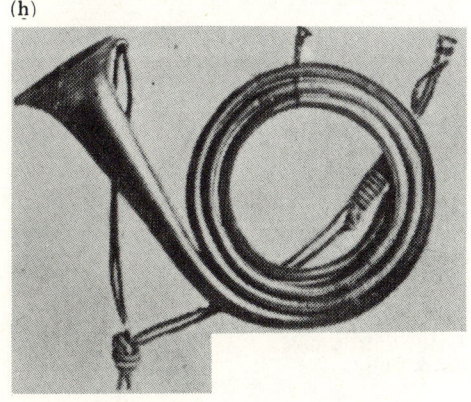
(h)

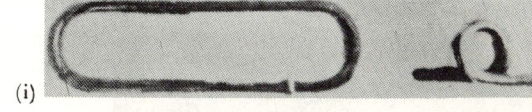
(i)

Figure 16
(a) *Copper and brass triple-coil horn in F (nearly ½ tone flat by modern standards) by Wm. Bull. Formerly in Galpin Collection, and now in Horniman Museum Carse Collection (Grove's Dictionary of Music, courtesy Macmillan & Co)*
(b) *Anonymous brass orchestral horn, probably English and late eighteenth century. Crooks of the early Viennese type. Horniman Museum Carse Collection (Grove's Dictionary of Music, courtesy Macmillan & Co)*
(c) *Inventionshorn, with tuning slide crooks (shown with E♮ crook) by J. E. Hăltenhof. Hanau am Main 1776. Paris Conservatoire (Grove's Dictionary of Music, courtesy Macmillan & Co)*
(d) *Cor-solo of brass, with silver mounts by Raoux, Paris. Shown with E♭ crook, Paris Conservatoire (Grove's Dictionary of Music, courtesy Macmillan & Co)*
(e) *Natural trumpet in D, J. W. Haas, Nuremberg, early eighteenth century (Grove's Dictionary of Music, courtesy of Macmillan & Co)*
(f) *Natural trumpet in F, Kerner, Vienna 1806, with crook (Grove's Dictionary of Music, courtesy Macmillan & Co)*
(g) *Slide trumpet in F, Harris, London 1730. Slide added later (Grove's Dictionary of Music, courtesy Macmillan & Co)*
(h) *Coiled natural trumpet in D, Pfeiffer, Leipzig 1697 (Grove's Dictionary of Music, courtesy Macmillan & Co)*
(i) *E♭ and C crooks for (g)*

partly because its new middle register had melodic limitations. As with the horn, its original pitch could be altered by the insertion of crooks. However, during this century there were determined efforts to increase its complete middle range. One idea was to make the trumpet in the shape of an arc so that the horn technique of lowering notes by inserting the hand into the bell ('stopping') could be applied. More successful attempts were the slide and keyed trumpets. The slide trumpet made use of a telescopic slide that lengthened the tube and therefore altered the fundamental pitch of a note, as the trombone still does. This sort of trumpet was popular in England at the end of the seventeenth century, but did not come in for intensive improvements until the beginning of the nineteenth century. The keyed trumpet and later valve trumpet appeared too late to be in the scope of this century.

The only other new instruments that you might not have met in the course up until now are the kettle-drums or timpani. Used as a pair at this time, they were introduced into Europe in the fifteenth century when it was usual to support trumpeters with a mounted kettle-drummer in the retinue. By the middle of the seventeenth century the kettle-drums had followed the trumpet into the orchestra in German church music, French ballet and Italian opera. The two drums were usually tuned a fourth apart, to tonic and lower dominant notes of the piece, and it was possible to tune them by hand by tightening the drum skin equally around the head of the instrument with a key.

Timpani of eighteenth-century from Johan Christoph Weigel's 'Musicalisches Theatrum' (Courtesy Bärenreiter & Co)

To sum up the importance of development during this period, with words of the German musicologist, Dr Friedrich Blume:

> The orchestra has been enlarged and strengthened since the Classic period, enriched by a few instruments, but basically not altered. The technique of orchestral playing, too, has remained unchanged, founded as it is on strict discipline, uniform bowing for strings, precise articulation by all instruments, and the merging of all into a perfectly homogeneous totality of sound (in contrast to the cleavages in late Baroque sonority). Johann Adolf Hasse and Johann Georg Pisendel in Dresden, Graun in Berlin, Stamitz and Cannabich in Mannheim, Jommelli in Stuttgart, Haydn in Eisenstadt and Esterház, and many others were severe trainers of their orchestras, the fruits of their labours have nourished two centuries, and today's perfectionism is nothing but the ultimate heightening of their technique.[1]

7.0 SOME TERMS RELATING TO STYLE

7.1 Ancient Classicism stressed balance, proportion, clarity, moderation and serenity. In the eighteenth century these ideals were admired by some (but not by others!) and a return to the spirit of them took place in architecture and the fine arts, and later in music. As the composer Gluck (1714–87) said: 'Music must show balance and order.' There was a need felt, also, to achieve universal understanding and sympathy.

7.2 The term 'Classical' in music came to refer to a style starting around 1740 with composers like Hasse, the opera composer who achieved such fame and influence at Dresden, Quantz, Domenico Scarlatti and J. S. Bach's sons. Professor Blume[2] sums up certain definitive characteristics of the new style:

> One aspect of the music at this time of importance, is that for the first time the idea that music was not obliged to entertain or be purpose composed in any way, but should be for its own sake. It coincides with a simplification of forms and stylistic means. The supreme Italian influence was rivalled by the growing importance of German instrumental music at the time. It became a time of continuous assimilation and interweaving of national contributions.

7.3 Classical style in music can be divided into two phases, the first from about 1740 to the 1770s, the second to the 1800s. The first includes the *galant* style, the *Empfindsamkeit* or 'sensibility' style and also briefly the so-called *Sturm und Drang* (Storm and Stress)[3] stage. The second might be called the 'high' Classical style. This was more resolved and constant, and because of this it left composers free within it to contribute and develop in their own way, as exemplified in the works of Mozart and middle and late Haydn.

7.4 *Galant* style and performance is best appreciated by examining an example of it. In Quantz's book on flute playing there is a flute adagio in two versions, the first plain and the second embellished. It is the embellished style of solo performance that qualifies the music for the description *galant*. A variety of new performance methods stand out: the range of dynamics is wide and they are

---

[1] From *Classic and Romantic Music* by Friedrich Blume, 1972.

[2] Friedrich Blume, *Classic and Romantic Music*.

[3] A202 Unit 12 *Goethe* discusses this at some length.

constantly changing; phrasing ranges from single staccato notes to long slurred cascades; as Leopold Mozart advises in his essay on violin method, chromatic notes and appoggiaturas are accented and embellishments in general are mercurial and sensitive in dynamic nuance. The whole effect is highly mannered, even sentimental, with its touches of melancholy. In the fifth edition of Grove's *Dictionary of Music and Musicians*, *galant* is described as

> a somewhat flatly and affectedly expressive style, not devoid of sensibility, but with little sensitiveness and no profoundity. The harmony is usually shallow and not especially interesting in itself; the melody is suave and dispassionate; and profuse ornamentation, carefully defined in a way amounting to a science, is the most prominent feature of the style.

7.5 *Empfindsamkeit* or 'sensibility' is not a contrast to *galant*, merely a stage of it. In the introduction to C. P. E. Bach's Essay, William Mitchell defines Bach's *Empfindsamkeit* thus:

> his music was a vehicle for the expression of the emotions. Music must languish, it must startle, it must be gay, it must move boldly from one sentiment to another and the performer must transmit accurately and faithfully its expressive nuances to the audience whose heart must be stirred. This is the parallel to *Sturm und Drang* [in literature].

7.6 *Empfindsamkeit* can be said to be characterized by emphasis on expression of sentiment, whereas one might possibly say that *Sturm und Drang* in music is characterized by emphasis on passion. The term *Sturm und Drang* took its name from a play by Klinger of 1776, so this term cannot really be applied before this time in literature, although the musical equivalent of this stage was certainly before this date. The idea associated with the movement was that personal freedom (chiefly that of the artist) should not be chained by restrictions of law or convention, and emotional intensity and passionate outbursts are characteristic of it.

7.7 As you can appreciate these terms within the early Classical period are all very hard to define. Indeed, people tend to use them differently and this adds to the confusion. However, I think it is reasonable to say that this first part of the Classic period up to the 1770s embraced a variety of refinements and developments of the *galant* style that originally was so closely associated with the Rococo in the other arts.

7.8 Musical language during this earlier period was remarkably stereotyped. Rameau's *Traité de l'harmonie* (Treatise on harmony) (1722) and *Demonstration du principe de l'harmonie* (Demonstration of harmonic principles) (1750) go to show the new interest in harmonic vocabulary and demonstrate the limitations of its resources. Melodies were remarkably anonymous and cadences were clichéd. This is not to say that exceptional men like Stamitz and young Haydn were not individual, but similar phrases, harmonizations and so on occur frequently in the music of different composers. It was not until the stabilization of language in 'high' Classicism that composers were free to become individuals and offer unique contributions.

This gradual change in emphasis throughout the period, from light-weight to serious and more substantial, is reflected in the growth of the symphony.

8.0 EARLY SYMPHONIES AND SYMPHONISTS

8.1 We have time in this block to study only half a dozen representative symphonies or symphonic movements. I shall confine this section, therefore, to generalities about the form and style of the early symphonists, and not include long lists of composers, or make reference to works that you have no chance of hearing. As with most art forms, the beginnings are intrinsically less rewarding than the mature creation, and early symphonies are not often played today, despite the eighteenth-century revival. However, for those of you who wish to follow up and make some further study of this subject, an appendix at the end lists early symphony composers and recordings of early symphonies that are currently available. There were innumerable symphonies written. Composers undoubtedly found the form of the symphony as a whole and the form within movements both satisfactory and pleasing, challenging yet liberating. Audiences found the shape, weight and variety of the symphony, and the novelty of the symphony orchestra, exciting.

8.2 Around 1750 a number of completely different and conflicting styles were to be heard in works by composers such as J. S. Bach, Gluck, Rameau, Bach's sons, Stamitz and Jommelli. National styles and influences were strong, but composers travelled widely, taking ideas and styles with them and assimilating new ones where they worked.

8.3 In Italy the string school of Corelli, Torelli and Vivaldi had built up a powerful tradition. They favoured string music with simple harmony, rich texture and contrapuntal interest. Their great asset was the gift of long, beautiful melodic writing, no doubt associated with their history of the production and performance of opera. Quantz maintains that the Italians write more for the connoisseur than the amateur. In composition, he maintains, they are:

> broad-minded, magnificent, lively, expressive, profound, lofty in their way of thinking, somewhat bizarre, free, forward, audacious, extravagant, occasionally careless in their meter [i.e. in word-setting]; at the same time, they are also singing, ingratiating, delicate, moving, and rich in invention.

8.4 The French, in composition, Quantz maintains are:

> lively, expressive, natural, pleasing and intelligible to the public, and more correct in their meter [i.e. word-setting] than the Italians; at the same time, they are neither profound nor bold but on the contrary very narrow-minded, servile, always the same, common-place in their way of thinking, dry in invention; they continually warm over the idea of their predecessors and write more for the amateur than for the connoisseur.

8.5 In England there were two distinct styles: the solid Baroque tradition of Handel and still practised by composers like Boyce, and the fashionable *galant* style popular with composers like Arne and Linley. Charles Cudworth sums up the English symphonic style in his Royal Musical Association paper 'English Eighteenth-century Symphonies'. He maintains that there was a distinctive English style of melody, 'brief, but often of haunting charm, usually displayed in the small-scale slow movements'; that English first movements were not fanatical in their use of sonata form, even after it had been introduced; and that forms used were variable and unusual; that middle movements were usually short and last movements usually a minuet or a lively dance-like Rondo. He adds that 'the English delighted in bassoon solos, and loved the rough vigour of solo horns, contrasted with oboes, or even clarinets, a legacy from the much-loved "Water-Musick" of the great Mr Handel'.

8.6 It was in Germany that the Classical style was stabilized and here that the new music emerged. In North Germany, at the court of Frederick the Great, Quantz and C. P. E. Bach were composing in the *galant* and *Empfindsamkeit* styles. Although the *galant* style was also popular in Mannheim when Stamitz first went there in 1743 he soon made his new ideas popular and delighted audiences with a freshness and breadth of conception. The term *style bourgeois* (in contrast to the *style galant*) is sometimes applied to the Mannheim style, and this description does seem to imply something of the fire, immediacy and drama of Mannheim, compared with the prettified pleasantries of *galant*. The Germans had a gift for assimilating other people's inclinations in taste.

Quantz, therefore, recommends a mixing of style as a recipe for arriving at music 'that will be accepted by many countries and recognized as good'. He describes such a 'mixed taste' as 'the present [1752] German taste'. He points out that everybody knows that Italian and French composers, singers and instrumentalists have been in service at various German courts for more than a century but that now Germans have visited Italy and France, adopted the taste of other countries and 'hit upon a mixture which has enabled them to write and to perform with success, not only German, but also Italian, French and English operas and other *Singspiele* [plays with singing], each in its own language and taste'. However, he is sure that when the Germans know how to select with due discrimination from the musical tastes of others, they will arrive at their own true taste, which, as it happened, turned out to be both successfully German and universal.

8.7 Early Classical symphonies might appear simple and even trivial to us (indeed some of them certainly are!), but that is partly due to the fact that we are standing beyond subsequent development. The process of the development of sonata form as the predominant and most important aspect of the first movement was slow but continuous. Early symphonic movements of Stamitz are in simple binary form, and early examples of sonata form scarcely contain a second theme of any distinct character, merely a definite move to the dominant. The addition of a fourth movement was haphazard, and the four-movement symphony was by no means standard even with early Mozart and Haydn. First movements were usually in $\frac{2}{2}$, $\frac{4}{4}$ or $\frac{3}{4}$ time and marked Allegro, or sometimes Presto or Vivace. An opening convention at Mannheim and in Paris was the *premier coup d'archet* (first stroke of the bow), a precision attack on the strings which Mozart tells us became a feature. Later in the symphony's evolution first movements are occasionally preceded by a slow introduction, but this is rare with the early symphonists. The slow movements are usually Andante or Andantino in $\frac{3}{8}$ or $\frac{2}{4}$ time, counted in quavers, and very often in binary form. Last movements in early symphonies are often minuets, although just as often marked Presto, Vivace or Allegro, in $\frac{3}{4}$ or $\frac{2}{4}$ time, and either in binary or simple rondo form.

8.8 Organic development in movements other than a first sonata-form movement was virtually unknown, and even in first movements development tends to be naïve, modest and short. Most symphonies written around 1770 were scored for first violins, second violins, violas, 'cellos and basses, two oboes and two horns. Flutes sometimes replaced oboes (often indeed played by the same musicians) and bassoons were used when they were available to double the bass line. Clarinets appeared infrequently, either replacing or doubling oboe parts.

When there were trumpeters and a timpanist at a musical establishment, parts for these players were provided. The continuo player who had filled out the harmonic texture became dispensable as inner strings and horns sustained the harmony, supplied volume and accentuated rhythms.

8.9 Adam Carse in his Royal Musical Association paper *Early Classical Symphonies* draws conclusions about the form and stylistic characteristics of the early symphony by investigation of 1,500 to 2,000 works which he found, mostly in manuscript parts, scattered in European libraries and museums[1]. Since sources for these works are so widely distributed, and so relatively few of them are available in printed form, I have drawn my generalizations from specialist authorities such as Dr Carse, while at the same time examining a good few of these early works.

However, as I said earlier, I don't think we can possibly appreciate the contribution of these pioneer symphonists without studying a selection, however arbitrary, of their work in some degree of detail and commitment.

9.0 HOW TO READ A SCORE

9.1 The scores of the symphonies that we shall be looking at become progressively more complex and so I thought a brief discussion of how to read a score might be useful.

Basically, of course, it is no different from following the scores of the Baroque music that you have been studying during the last few weeks, but there are a few differences. For one thing, there are more instruments involved. There are more performance directions and there is also the question of horns and trumpets being transposing instruments. Moreover, this music is stylistically very different and parts of melodic and harmonic importance tend to move about more quickly and be passed from one group of instruments to another. In fact rests are as important as notes in this music and texture is a changeable element.

9.2 Although there are more instruments, they are always arranged in the same family groups, and these are arranged basically in descending order of pitch. The woodwind family is on top, although the bassoon part is occasionally added to the general bass part in scores of this period, when it is not so very different from them. The brass instruments (horns and trumpets) come next and then the timpani if necessary. Finally at the bottom comes the string family with cellos and double-basses often sharing a stave.

---

[1] Egon Wellesz and Frederick Steinfeld, in *The Age of Enlightenment 1745–1790*, New Oxford History of Music, Vol. VII, suggest 'that well over 7,000 symphonies (or overtures used in concerts) dating from the period 1740–1816 are still extant and there is evidence of many more that have disappeared.'

SYMPHONY No. 104 "The London"

J. Haydn

9.3 Performance directions you can look up in *A New Dictionary of Music*, or else in the Introduction to Music units of A100, where they are explained in principle if not in entirety. Most of the dynamic marks are degrees of *piano* (quietly) and *forte* (loudly) with subtleties such as *rinforzando* or *sforzando* or *fortepiano* (*fp*) which concern sudden accents.

Other directions such as staccato and pizzicato concern the manner of playing.

Slurring and phrasing are self-evident and very important since they can affect the whole nature and sound of a melody. Composers at this time were beginning to mark exactly how they wanted things to sound.

9.4 I've already discussed horns and trumpets and their limitations and mentioned the fact that crooks were added to give them a new fundamental and consequent range of possible notes, thus basing them in one of several keys. The brass player, however, read all the parts with the same embouchure or lip-pressure[1] in C major, and the addition of the necessary crook did the transposing for him. We therefore find that all horn and trumpet parts of this time are written in C major, but marked for horns or trumpets in D or whatever the key of the movement happens to be. This means that when a horn player reads and applies the necessary lip-pressure for C, his instrument will sound D; if he has his F crook and plays C the actual sound would be F, and so on.

I don't think it is necessary to worry about this problem. If you want to work out exactly what notes the instruments are actually sounding you can transpose the written part at the appropriate distance. Otherwise it is easy to see the melodic shape and rhythmic emphasis of the part and realize that it is in harmony with the other parts round about it.

9.5 Don't forget that :|| is a repeat sign and means turning back in the music, either to the beginning or else to ||: or to a sign of some sort, commonly 𝄋 (D.S. means return *dal segno*, i.e. to the sign).

10.0 CASE STUDY I

Sammartini: Symphony in G major, before 1744. Milan (1st movement).

Giovanni Battista Sammartini (Liceo Musicale G. B. Martini Bologna; Photo. Fotofast)

---

[1] It is with lip-pressure that the player can control the production of notes of the harmonic series.

10.1 Giovanni Battista Sammartini was the younger brother of Giuseppe Sammartini the oboist and composer who spent much of his working life in London. Giovanni Battista Sammartini was born in Milan in about 1700 and remained there all his life, apart from visits to other European centres for musical events. He gained a reputation originally as a composer of church music, then gradually became interested in instrumental music and turned his attention to the symphony, which was then in about 1730 in its early stages of growth. Not only was the school of symphony composers he headed one of the earliest, it was also the only Italian-based one. His first symphony in 1734 was well received in Milan.

> It was an outstanding success and became all the rage in that large capital, where music is held to be a very agreeable pastime. Count Palfi (Pálffy), grand chancellor of Hungary, Count Schönborn and Count Mortzin rivalled each other in obtaining the latest compositions of Sammartini which were heard almost every day at their concerts.[1]

In fact, Sammartini became so celebrated a composer that he was much in demand as a teacher also. He taught Gluck for four years from 1737 to 1741. He died in 1775.

10.2 Although Georges de Saint-Foix produced his 'La Chronologie de l'oeuvre instrumentale de Jean-Baptiste Sammartini' (The chronology of Jean-Baptiste Sammartini's instrumental work) in 1914,[2] and more recent scholars such as Newell Jenkins, Jan La Rue and Bathia D. Churgin have done a great deal of work classifying, editing and analysing, surprisingly few of Sammartini's works are published. However, his complete output is thought to number more than 2,000, including 77 symphonies. Charles Burney, while visiting Milan, heard Sammartini play at the keyboard and said that he had 'a way peculiar to himself of touching that instrument which [was] truly masterly and pleasing'. This gift he also applied to his symphonic writing.

10.3 As a symphony composer Sammartini can be considered a later representative of the Italian violin school of Vivaldi that you have been studying, a contemporary of Jommelli and precursor of Galuppi and Boccherini. He was successful as a symphonist because, although he had the Italian gift for elegant and graceful melody, and sensitive embellishment, he was not so preoccupied with the melodic line that he lost his sense of balance and proportion. His works were performed abroad, in Amsterdam in 1738 (by Vivaldi) and in 1751 in Paris under the patronage of La Pouplinière. In England he was also popular and it is even possible that some of his works were published there under his brother's name. He collaborated with Jommelli over two cantatas in 1753, and must have known J. C. Bach during the latter's employment as cathedral organist in Milan between 1755 and 1762. Boccherini and Mozart both knew him and his work in Milan.

10.4 There has been considerable confusion about the instrumental music of Sammartini. Georges de Saint-Foix claimed that many of the works attributed to his brother Giuseppe and published in Paris were in actual fact by Giovanni Battista Sammartini. Henry G. Mistikin in 'The Published Instrumental Works of Giovanni Battista Sammartini: A Bibliographical Reappraisal'[3] maintains that this was a publisher's error and the works in question are by two very different composers. He cites op. 1 as representing two distinct styles—one the

[1] Carpani: *Le Haydine* (Milan 1812)

[2] In *Sammelbande der Internationalen Musik—Gesellschaft XV* (1914)

[3] In *The Musical Quarterly* of 1959 (vol. 45).

old-fashioned four-movements type (slow–fast–slow–fast) with allegros in Baroque counterpoint and the other the three-movement plan of the Neapolitan opera overture—as is the symphony we shall study. In fact all the symphonies now attributed to Giovanni Sammartini begin with a fast movement. The styles are distinct, and the conclusion is that Giovanni Battista began his career in the new *galant* style in which he was immediately confident and secure. I think our musical case study illustrates this in some measure, although it is a relatively early work.

10.5 The symphony in G major which we are to study was first published in Paris in 1744 and is scored for strings alone. Originally this symphony had probably only three movements, ending with a typical finale in $\frac{3}{8}$ time. A minuet borrowed from an early Sammartini trio sonata was added as a fourth movement by one early copyist, and this is often included in performance. **Play the first movement** and consider the opening page of score.

Exercise

Can you recognize any characteristics, either Baroque or *galant*, in the string writing, typical of the concerti grossi you have been studying in previous units—typical sequential clichés, ornaments, cadences, bass lines, figurations and so on?

Discussion

You probably noticed the following points:

(i) Characteristic Baroque method of keeping the opening busy and exciting despite static harmony.

(ii) Characteristic *galant* cadential bar at the last half beat of bar 3 to the third beat of bar 4, and again at the last half beat of bar 4 to the third of bar 5, consisting of a tie over the bar in the melody, followed by a falling sixth and a feminine cadence (that is the final note not on the accent):

(iii) Sequential figuration between the upper two strings at bars 6 and 7 with a typical 'circle of fifths' bass parts as below:

One might call these features clichés, but even this cannot detract from the spontaneous vitality, expansive sonority and graceful lines, in which the contrast of stepwise movement and telling leaps is so skilfully balanced. If you look at the score you will see that this movement is in two sections, the second longer than the first, and each repeated. I don't have to tell you that this makes it look like the familiar Baroque binary form. However, half-way through the second half at bar 34 we find ourselves faced with a recapitulation of the opening in the tonic and recognize at bar 46 onward certainly more than a confirmation of this tonality. With a definite move to D major, the dominant of G major, at bar 12 (by means of a typically *galant* cadence, incidentally) and a repetition of this section in G major at bar 46, these last bars possibly take on the character of more than an extended cadential figure—an embryo second subject; in other words, the movement is in a definite, although simple, sonata form.

There is one other section that I'd especially like to point your attention to. It's at the beginning of the second part, bars 21–4, where Sammartini draws out his original cadential sequences in a subtle and extended way to move to E minor for the beginning of a more exciting 'development' that leads up to the recapitulation.

Exercise

Can you suggest what techniques Sammartini uses to heighten tension in this second section, especially between bars 25 and 33?

Discussion

I hope you may have discovered some of the following points.

(i) Constant moving bass, with quaver movement accelerating to semiquavers.

(ii) Harmony in upper parts changing over a bass part which lags behind, moving on the following beat.

(iii) A similar effect a few bars later (bars 27–32) where the two violin parts force each other down with 'suspensions'.

(iv) More interesting and possibly surprising harmonic moves—especially in bars 29 and 31.

Exercise

Play this movement through a few times, and consider the following questions:

(i) What contributes to the feeling of unity in this movement?
(ii) Are there moments of surprise, or do you anticipate the steps it takes?

As a symphony, this example by Sammartini is obviously of a rudimentary nature. It is, however, important for a number of reasons. I have drawn your attention to a variety of features that you recognize from your studies of the last few weeks. Sammartini certainly uses a language familiar to you. But the symphony's importance is that it points forward to things to come. You have only the score and recording of the first movement and it is difficult for you therefore to evaluate the whole. However, certain differences from Baroque chamber music stand out. The Sammartini movement shares the same energy and expansiveness but on the whole it is more closely structured and more complex. The graceful Italian violin melodies are evident but there is less ornamentation of the melodic line and more sense of direction. The writing contains less imitative counterpoint, and unity and purpose are achieved by new means.

11.0 **CASE STUDY 2**

Wagenseil: Symphony D major, 1746. Vienna (1st movement).

11.1 George Christoph Wagenseil was born in Vienna in 1715. After serving as a singing boy in the chapel of the Dowager Empress Wilhelmena Amalia, he began studying law (like a number of other composers), but changed his mind and turned to music, studying under J. J. Fux, the eminent Viennese composer and theorist, and Matteo Palotta. He became court composer in 1739, and from 1741 was also chapel organist to the Dowager Empress Elizabeth Christine. After his first Italian visit in 1745 for the performance of his opera *Ariodante* in Venice, he was appointed court 'klavier meister' (keyboard master) since he was also a virtuoso performer. In fact in 1756 he obtained leave to make a concert tour. During the course of his travels, which lasted two years, he met the famous librettist Metastasio and impressed him with his keyboard playing and composition. Between 1759 and 1766 he was busy in Milan and met J. C. Bach. He had some influence on young Mozart, after Leopold Mozart, impressed with Wagenseil's compositions, brought his son to see him in Vienna

Johann Christoph Wagenseil 1633–1708, engraving by Jakob Sandrart 1690 (Archiv für Kunst und Geschichte, Berlin)

in 1762 and 1768. Wagenseil had started having some sort of circulatory trouble with the fingers of his left hand, and when this spread to his right hip he was unable to leave his room, and consequently was obliged to give up his official appointments. However, he composed more than ever and gave lessons in composition and keyboard playing. He died in Vienna in 1777.

11.2 Historically, Wagenseil's importance is due to a great extent to the fact that he was the most influential of the first school of symphony composers in Vienna, and therefore formed the immediate background to the work of Haydn, Mozart and Beethoven, the composers of the great Classical school. He inherited the form and idiom of symphonic writing of the Italians but injected a native quality into it, making the whole more closely knit and characteristically Austrian. The step taken by Wagenseil (and by Stamitz at the same time) concerned the construction and nature of his themes. Wagenseil's themes were constructed of independent motifs, capable of a more symphonic treatment and development. The themes became important in themselves as vehicles for ideas and this was an important step in the evolution of the early symphony. Wagenseil's most important contribution, apart from this, was perhaps his symphonic atmosphere: the deliberate opposition of major and minor and his obvious feeling for harmonic colour give us a direct preview of the excitement and drama of the Classical symphony.

11.3 Wagenseil wrote a great deal of church and theatre music, instrumental music such as divertimentos, concertos for flute and keyboard and eighty-seven symphonies. For the most part the symphonies are in three movements, Allegro (or Vivace or Spiritoso), Andante (or Largo) and Presto (or Allegro assai). He usually wrote for strings with horns, but the symphony in D that we shall look at is more fully scored for strings, oboes and horns or trumpets with drums. This is because it was the opera symphony to *La Clemenza di Tito* (The Clemency of Titus) and larger orchestras were generally maintained in opera houses. The oboe part is somewhat primitive, and hardly used specifically for its tone quality. However in the slow movement flutes are substituted for oboes as having a possibly sweeter, gentler tone. The same players probably took both oboes and flutes in the orchestra as was the custom. The movements are Allegro, Andante and Tempo di Minuetto.

Remember that this is one of Wagenseil's earliest symphonies, and the generalizations I have just made about him were not necessarily yet evident. *On paper* this opening looks not so very different from the Sammartini first movement.

Title page of Wagenseil's MSS of Symphony in D major, Codex 17170. (Österreichische Nationalbibliothek Musiksammlung)

Exercise

Play the opening, and follow the score. In general impression, why is it so different *to listen to* from the Sammartini?

Discussion

Two things mainly I think: mood and orchestration. The mood is much more aggressive, and demands immediately an intense concentration. It is obviously not just the three-chord opening. Sammartini's opening is similar, but makes less demand. Wagenseil's opening puts one in mind of the commanding, authoritative openings of later symphonies by Haydn, Mozart and even Beethoven. The orchestration is more pungent. (Remember the Sammartini piece was scored for strings alone.) The traditional horn call (we chose trumpets for the recording) is held together by strong string chords powerful in their wide spacing and by rhythmic drumming. Notice how we are cut off short in the third bar.

This is a decisive opening that is achieved by well-considered orchestral means and not by chance.

Immediately, however, in the seventh bar we are plunged into a short section that modulates by changing the harmony bar by bar, and at the same time keeps interest by means of a motor rhythm.

This device for gradual and satisfactory modulation is typical of the Baroque in the way it's used to move the music from one tonality to another. Yet it points forward also to the Classical period in its poise and in the way it plays tonal games with the listener in its cadential bars, where five bars of tonic and dominant are alternated.

The new idea, when it comes on strings alone, takes us by surprise. We had moved, as expected, to the dominant key, to A major. The new idea, made up of two contrasting little phrases, begins immediately in A minor. The first of these motifs in unison is contrasted with a figure of descending chords on the violins.

This second figure is extended and ends brusquely in bar 24 with a return of the first motif of this second subject. Immediately in bar 26 we are off on busy violin figurations for a brief 'development'.

Exercise

The development is slight, but Wagenseil does expand each of his ideas to some extent. Can you identify the material he uses at:

(i) Bars 26–34.
(ii) Bars 34–8.
(iii) Bars 38–44.

Answer

(i) Bridge passage, opening figuration and tonic-dominant cadence figure.
(ii) First subject.
(iii) Second subject.

This section contains a number of interesting features which are characteristic of Wagenseil's attitude and which contribute to his importance in the symphony's development. His concept of sonorities is obviously orchestral, and he makes as much use as possible of contrast and more idiomatic instrumental writing. For example the trumpets are introduced in a sparing manner at moments when they can emphasize the rhythm and add volume and excitement to climaxes. Although the oboes are used to double the violins to a great extent, occasionally they sustain the harmony through the bar (as in bars 26 and 27) while the strings are busy with figurations of their own.

In quiet string passages Wagenseil frequently omits the lower strings for contrast of volume and timbre. He is very obviously aware of his orchestral means and does his best to exploit them albeit in a primitive manner. His themes are constructed of short but memorable motifs which offer the possibility of development. In all these ways this symphonic movement is forward-looking. The recapitulation is unremarkable but there is a vigorous coda.

12.0 CASE STUDY 3

Stamitz: Symphony in E♭, about 1755. Mannheim (1st movement).

12.1 Johann Wenzel Anton Stamitz (Jan Vázlav Antonin Stamic) was born in Německý (now Brod, eighty miles south-east of Prague), Bohemia in 1717. His father was organist of the local church and a composer of church music. Johann was the eldest of eleven children, all of whom were artistic in some way or another. He obviously got to know both native local music and Italian music in the church, and orchestral music from the nearby orchestras of Count Morzin and Count Questenberg. After attending a local Jesuit school, his horizons were broadened by a stay in Prague. Musical education in Bohemia was available to all school children and Dr Burney wrote,[1] after visiting schools there, that the Bohemians were 'perhaps the most musical nation in the whole of Europe'. Of Stamitz he wrote:

> he was educated in an ordinary town school among boys of ordinary talents, who lived and died as unknown creatures. But he, like a second

[1] *Diary of a Musical Journey.*

Shakespeare, overcame all obstacles and thus, as the eye of the former perceived all of nature, so did the latter elevate art ever further, without deviating from nature, as no one had done before him. His genius was original, bold and powerful; the inventiveness, fire and contrasts in the rapid tempo, the tender, charming and delicate melody in the slow movements, wittily joined together with a richness of accompaniment, characterize his works. All are full of significance conceived by the enthusiasm of a great mind, refined by culture without being stifled by it.

JAN·V·STAMIC·1717·1757

Jan Vaclar Antonin Stamic (Stamitz) 1717–1757, engraving from title page of 'L'Art du Violon' B. Cartier 1801 (State Library of Czech Socialist Republic)

His ambition as a youth was to become a virtuoso violinist. At the coronation celebrations of Emperor Charles VIII in Frankfurt-on-the-Main in 1742 he was described as 'the famous Virtuoso Stamitz'. From here, his first visit to Germany, he went straight to Mannheim into the service of Karl Philipp the Elector. After only a year this elector died, and was succeeded by Karl Theodor, who was to have such an effect on the music making of his court. Stamitz became first court violinist. He wrote music for the theatre, chapel, symphonic and chamber concerts, and attended to music at the summer palace of Schwetzingen. The orchestra at Mannheim consisted of 50 players, and in 1750 he became instrumental music director there. In 1751 and 1754 he visited Paris, where he was already well known as a symphonist by reputation. During the 1754–5 Paris season the publisher Bayard brought out a series of symphonies under the collective title *La Melodia Germanica*. This very title acknowledged the existence of a German school of symphonists, and indeed the French recognized the importance and superiority of the German symphonists. Several of Stamitz's symphonies, including the one we shall be looking at, were in this collection. Stamitz died in 1757 at Mannheim.

12.1 In Johann Stamitz, the eighteenth century saw an outstanding virtuoso orchestra leader, and a disciplinarian comparable in influence on orchestral playing generally with Lully in the previous century. His orchestra developed style and virtuosity, experimenting with tonal colours and dramatic dynamics. Whereas in Baroque music dynamics had been used as contrast in the structure between tutti and solo groups, or for echo effects, with Stamitz it became an independent expressive feature. It added both to overall structure of a movement (for example a crescendo building up to a recapitulation) and to the dramatic effect (for example a *piano* motif repeated suddenly *forte*—one of Haydn's favourite devices). He revolutionized treatment of the sequence. Many of his bridge passages and development sections are built up of sequential development which became at the same time an instrument of expression and tension. Gradually under him at Mannheim the harpsichord became dispensable as a continuo instrument and the orchestra became independent of it. Sonata form took root and flourished. He was responsible for a great many achievements and his influence lasted several generations.

12.3 Altogether he wrote about 175 works, including some church music, some solo concertos and seventy-four symphonies. There is no information about the chronology of Stamitz's works and the only way of dating them is by stylistic characteristics. His chamber and symphonic works, however, fall into two main periods: an early one up until around 1745, which is characterized by themes of an Italian character, and the later period, which is distinguished by its energetic and positive approach, and the use of more contrast and finer nuances.

In the symphonies of the early period strings only are used, and later horns were added. One early characteristic which is possibly Neapolitan in derivation is a liking for syncopated themes.

Symphony in G   etc.

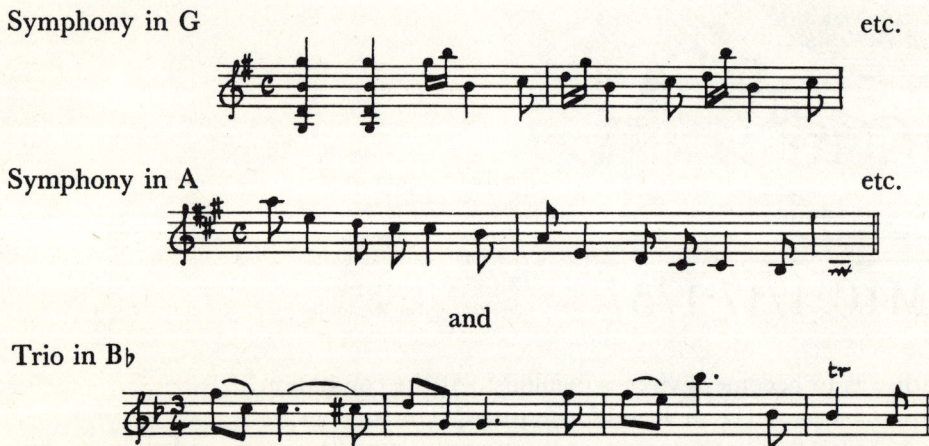

Symphony in A   etc.

and

Trio in B♭

There is certainly no doubt about the Italian influence in these early works. From the first Stamitz aimed at strong broad effects rather than detail. The conditions and demands at Mannheim were stimulating, and there was every temptation and encouragement to experiment and develop both the resources and the forms available to him. In his more native works therefore, certain stylistic finger-prints became recognizable.

The first subjects of his later sonata-form movements are composed of short motifs, each easily recognizable and often emphatic.

Symphony in D (i)

Symphony in D (ii)

Bursts of dynamic sound, carefully notated, produce an exciting effect.

Symphony in D (iii)

and
Symphony in E♭

His second subjects are contrasted with the first, often of a sweet and cantabile nature, and usually in the dominant or relative key.

The development sections exploit dynamic contrast, rhythmic and harmonic variety and the famous Mannheim crescendo. Whereas in the earlier works the treatment of wind instruments had been simple and relatively uninteresting, either doubling the strings or providing sustained harmony, they later became liberated, valued in their own right for their different sound qualities and contrasted or added to one another. The bass line also gains independence. The slow movement themes remain Italianate although one glimpses the Classical slow movement to come.

Symphony in E♭

The Minuet and Trio and the quicker, often more light-weight last movements provided ample scope for contrast and brilliance.

There is no doubt that the years around 1750 were a transitional period stylistically and formally. And Stamitz made an important and long-lasting contribution to the development of the new style of composition, orchestration and form.

12.4 Stamitz was a pioneer. Formally and orchestrally, he had little to build on and much of his work was innovatory. The form of this first movement might be described as unusual and experimental. I'd like to give you a rough breakdown of its sonata-form components and then ask your reaction to this treatment of other problems such as use of orchestra, shape and character of the music and so on. Here is the plan. You will notice that the form of the movement is irregular, but not, I think, unsatisfactory.

Bar	Key	Code	Role
1	E♭	a^1	1st subject group
5		a^2	
11		a^3	
18		a^4	
23		(a^3)	
27		b^1	Bridge
31	B♭	b^2	
39		(a^2)	
47		c^1 with c^2	2nd subject
66		a^4	Development
71		a^3	
78	E♭	b^2	
	F mi ⎫ all closely		
	G mi ⎬ related		
	C mi ⎭ keys		
90	E♭	b^1	
92		b^2	
100	in E♭ *on* a B♭ bass	a^2	Recapitulation
108		c^1, c^2	
127		a^4	Coda
132		a^2	
139		a^1	

Play the recording of this movement and follow your score. It abounds in examples of those characteristics that make Stamitz significant. What characteristics? Jot down your ideas under the following headings:

(i) Nature of themes.
(ii) Use of devices such as tremolo, crescendo and characteristic figurations.
(iii) Orchestration.
(iv) General style.

Discussion
(i) The first subject can be divided into four motifs, which are each quite different and easily identifiable, and which offer scope for development. The second subject is more extended and of a more lyrical nature.
(ii) After the opening flourishes a crescendo is built up gradually between bars 18 and 23. It uses both a measured tremolo (in the second violins and violas in bar 19), and held wind notes, and breaks out into its climax with a characteristic horn call on the horns, oboes and second violins.
(iii) In his use of the orchestra, he fully exploits natural instrumental possibilities. The strings use the full range of their expressiveness, both in more sustained melody and in atmosphere building techniques such as tremolo. The horns use their characteristic motif. The oboes are highlighted as soloists in the second subject with a detached string and horn accompaniment.

(iv) We are a long way from the Baroque concerto grosso style. The immediate introduction of several different ideas, the use of colour and dynamic effect—in fact the whole breadth of conception is of a new order.

Fétis, the Belgian historian and critic writing in the nineteenth century, describes Stamitz thus:

> Gifted with an original genius, he put a brilliance and lightness into his music more than could be found in the works of his German contemporaries. His symphonies preceded Haydn's and perhaps they were not without some influence on the development of that man's genius.

13.0 CASE STUDY 4

C. P. E. Bach. Symphony in D major, 1775. Hamburg

Carl Philip Emmanuel Bach
(National Library Budapest)

13.1 Carl Philipp Emanuel Bach was born at Weimar in 1714, the fifth child of J. S. Bach. He studied law at Leipzig University for three years before going on to Frankfurt-on-the-Oder to further his studies and support himself. He left there in 1738 and moved to Berlin, hoping to find work there. However, just at this this time he was summoned to Rheinsberg by the heir to the Prussian throne, Crown Prince Friedrich, who had gathered a great many musicians around him so that he could enjoy his favourite pastime—he was a keen amateur flute player. C. P. E. Bach was engaged as an accompanist. Two years later Prince Friedrich became king (to be known later as Frederick the Great) and moved to Berlin. Here Bach's colleagues among others were the famous flautist, Johann Joachim Quantz, who was the king's teacher, the brothers Graun and the brothers Benda. C. P. E. Bach himself at this time occupied a very modest position compared with some of these, and unfortunately did not possess the natural traits of character that might have made his position more acceptable to him. He found it difficult to defer to the king in matters of musicianship and taste, to pretend responses he did not experience, and he had a caustic tongue that he could not always restrain. Relations between them were not of the best, nor did the king appreciate the modern, progressive character of Bach's music. It is difficult to imagine why C. P. E. Bach did not leave and accept another position—he had many offers. It might have been because although he himself was a Saxon subject, his wife and three children were Prussians, and the king had the right to detain any of his subjects if he wished, or perhaps the king would not release Bach himself. And the atmosphere in Berlin was artistically most stimulating. The town was full of scholars and writers. Several treatises on musical theory were published from here at this time by Marpurg, Quantz, Agricola and C. P. E. Bach himself. By now he had a considerable reputation as one of the finest keyboard players in Germany, and when after the Seven Years' War (1756–63) Frederick had less resources and enthusiasm for music-making, Bach applied for and was successful in obtaining the post of musical director left vacant by the death of his godfather and friend Telemann in Hamburg. He moved in 1768. His new job entailed being Cantor of the Latin school and musical director of Hamburg's five churches. Here he flourished, seemingly enjoying the vast amount of organizing and administration, conducting and composing, himself seeing to instrumentalists, vocalists, copyists and so on, and being obliged to provide an enormous amount of music for performance, either newly composed or by composers such as Telemann and his father J. S. Bach. The job was well paid, and he was happy amid a wide circle of friends, among whom were the writers Lessing and Klopstock.

Apart from his 'bread-and-butter' work, as he called it, he spent his time composing for his own pleasure, improvising (according to all accounts he was marvellous at it!), and concert giving as conductor and sololist. When he died in 1788 his obituary in the Hamburg press stated:

> He was one of the greatest theoretical and practical musicians, creator of true clavier technique ... unmatched on this instrument. Music loses in him one of its greatest ornaments and to musicians the name of Carl Philipp Emanuel Bach will always be a holy one. In his personal intercourse he was a lively, cheerful man, full of spirit and wit, gay and merry ...

His musical career can be divided into three periods: the first in which he was obviously influenced by his father's Baroque style, especially in his use of sequences, Baroque cadences and step-wise bass lines; the second in Berlin, where he grew to maturity and where his music became more powerful, emotional and subjective; and the third when he reached his compositional peak in Hamburg. Here he became a recognized leader both in language and style, and was admired by Haydn and Mozart. We now call his compositions of this Hamburg period his *Sturm and Drang*[1] works, since they are characterized by the same turbulence and emotion as the early Romantic play of that name.

13.2 He was a prolific composer. He wrote more than a hundred keyboard sonatas and many other keyboard works, a quantity of chamber music, concertos, vocal music, both sacred and secular, and eighteen symphonies. Although in a way he is not typical of the *galant* style of his time in its tendency to superficiality and shallowness, nevertheless he does represent a musical parallel to the great *Sturm and Drang* literary figures. In emotional intensity and meaningful subjectivity he had a powerful and influential effect on the next generation of symphony composers—on Haydn, Mozart and Beethoven, although his contribution was only one element in the evolution of Classical style.

---

[1] As I've already mentioned, this is discussed in A202 Unit 12, *Goethe*.

13.3 The symphony in D major is one of four symphonies written in Hamburg between 1775 and 1776 and published with a dedication to Prince Friedrich Wilhelm of Prussia in 1780. Eight symphonies from the Berlin period exist, but in different versions. Of the ten symphonies written in Hamburg the first six of 1773 were composed for Gottfried van Swieten, Austrian ambassador to the Court at Berlin,[1] and are scored for strings and continuo—almost a return to the concerto symphony of the early part of the century. The last four are dedicated to the Crown Prince and are scored for two flutes, two oboes, two horns, strings, bassoon and cembalo continuo, and are in the traditional three movements, fast–slow–fast.

Allegro di molto

The first of the four Hamburg symphonies shows much of the powerful interest and appeal of the *Sturm and Drang* style. Its first movement, in sonata form, begins in a most unusual way, quite dissimilar from the characteristic attention–demanding opening of the Mannheimers. Immediately an atmosphere of turbulence, unrest and anticipation is established by the string section alone with repeated notes in the first violin part accompanied by irregular erratic unison arpeggio figures on the lower strings. The first violin part is interesting and unusual in its decreasing rhymths.

As the full woodwind joins in with syncopated chording the tension mounts to a climax at bar 24 with a modulation to E minor. The transition period that follows makes use both of repeated sustained notes and the moving arpeggio figure, introducing its final shift to A major with a quieter, more sustained passage for two oboes and quietly moving bassoon—an exposed passage with gently flowing contrapuntal interest. By bar 44 we are definitely in the dominant. Here the violins enter with repeated Es, reminiscent of their opening figuration, to accompany a brief but unusual passage for flutes. These exposed woodwind passages, and there are several in this movement, have a serenity and tranquillity about them that is rare, and that gives us a foretaste of Beethoven. The mood at this point (bar 49) does not last long, and we are plunged into a section in the minor that makes use of syncopated wind chords, arpeggio figurations and a new rhythmic motif

which is passed between the woodwind. The violins are busy and restless and the tonality shifting and insecure.

Exercise

Play the exposition over several times (until bar 71). How do you regard this as an exposition? That is bearing in mind the qualities that have become established and accepted, and necessary for the presentation of balanced and contrasted musical ideas. Comment very briefly under the headings of:

(i) Nature of subjects (are they clearcut, predictable, contrasted etc.?).
(ii) Formal structure (is this a characteristic example of sonata form?).
(iii) Key scheme (is the tonal development expected?).

---

[1] Mainly remembered today as the librettist of Haydn's oratorio *The Creation* (1798).

Discussion

The whole of the exposition is unusual and displays few of the characteristics that we have discussed as being essential to sonata form. The first subject is somewhat indecisive—certainly it has no main tune or obvious shape. The transition is not at all direct, and meanders before reaching the second subject, which is itself unusual. After the four bars of flute thirds in A major this plunges into A minor with figures deriving from the first subject. The key scheme is unexpected. We touch on the flat side (with a c♮) in the fourth bar, end the first subject in E minor, move through quite remote keys in the course of the second subject, yet begin the development section (in bar 72) back in the dominant.

What is there, then, about this movement that is so powerful and compelling? If we look at the rest of the movement, we can see what Bach intends to do with an exposition of this nature. In the development section which follows he uses the fragmented and angular outline of the themes and the rapid tonal transitions in a masterly and compelling way. What a surprise his contemporary audience must have received at bar 79 with unexpected c♮s and a sudden plunge from D major to F major, which is three degrees flatter! Throughout this section there is a great deal of contrapuntal interest, and independent motifs of significance are developed simultaneously—for instance at bars 90–101.

The introduction of the transition material for two oboes and bassoon gives us a moment of repose and poise. From bar 108 onward the flutes and oboes transcend the independent string part to ride above it with charm and self-sufficiency. The solo passages from bar 122 to the recapitulation (bar 136) show a Beethovenian mastery of economy and drama. The exposed contrast of solo groups and spareness of the arpeggio string figure which is passed from one instrument to another provokes an energetic burst of A major figuration (A major being the dominant of D where the recapitulation will begin).

The recapitulation, beginning at bar 136, takes a strange turn at the end. After an unexpected subdominant touch at bar 209 (with a C♮ in the bass part), just as we think we're touching down for the final cadence the bass drops dramatically one semitone from B to B♭ in bar 211, while the upper strings move to a dominant seventh chord on it, finally cadencing gently in E♭ in readiness for the second movement which is in E♭ major. This choice of key for the slow movement is decidedly odd.

Exercise

Describe the orchestration and texture of the Largo. Why does Bach choose the instrumentation he does?

Discussion

This charming interlude is almost a pastoral for two flutes (doubled on solo viola and 'cello, two octaves below) and unsupported bass (originally violone). The composer marks the bass part *senza cembalo* (that is, without harpsichord) and the texture is consequently thin and widely spaced. The occasional violin pizzicato links add an extra tone colour but they are used sparingly and always alone.

Although Bach has chosen to limit his tone qualities in this way, by spacing the two tonal groups widely apart he has drawn attention to their individual beauty. The movement is quiet, serene and entirely without any undercurrent of tension. The independent bass part is sparse, and moments of remarkable beauty occur when the two melodic lines join into unison for a bar or so and then split up to harmonize a cadence, as in bars 13 to 14 and 17 to 19. Perhaps it is because the doubling is at a distance of two octaves that such a special tranquillity is achieved. Whatever, it looks forward to some of the slow movement writing of Beethoven. Finally it cadences imperfectly on an A major chord which leads immediately to the final Presto.

13.5 The Presto movement is a complete contrast to the other two movements—lively, vigorous and uninhibited. Its impetus carries it along at a fast pace, only occasionally checked by touches of humour such as this passage. If you play this movement through from the beginning you will notice a change of movement, sonority and volume at this point.

Exercise

What makes these bars such a surprise?

༺༺

Discussion

1 The use of pauses and bars of silence.
2 The change from full orchestra to strings.
3 The change from full texture to unisons.
4 The change from *forte* to *piano*.
5 The touches of chromaticism.

The movement is conservative in form. It is in the two-part binary form so familiar to us in J. S. Bach, Domenico Scarlatti and their contemporaries. Both halves, as usual, are repeated and there is a brief coda.

14.0 CASE STUDY 5

J. C. Bach. Symphony op. 18. no. 4. in D major, 1781. London.

14.1 Johann Christian Bach was born in 1735 and was the youngest son of Johann Sebastian Bach. His father died when he was fifteen, and he went to live with his elder half-brother Carl Philipp Emanuel Bach (whose music we've just been studying), who guided his musical education. Berlin at this time was full of opportunities to hear chamber music and opera and Johann Christian no doubt benefited from them all. When he was twenty he left his family for Italy, where he called himself Giovanni Bach, learned to speak fluent Italian, and became a member of the Roman Catholic church. Under the patronage of Count Litta of Milan he continued his composition studies most successfully with Giovanni Battista (Padre) Martini of Bologna, the eminent scholar and theorist. In 1760 he became organist of Milan cathedral, but continually visited Naples to hear the opera, since his overwhelming interest was in dramatic music. He began to make a name for himself in this field and received commissions from the Teatro di San Carlo in Naples. After a year's absence from his post in Milan he was urged to return, but by that time his reputation had spread abroad, and he was invited to be official composer to the King's Theatre, London, by Colomba Mattei, the impresario. This was in 1762. Although Bach's official contract was not renewed beyond the first year, since Colomba Mattei returned to Italy, Bach (Burney tells us he called himself John Bach) was fruitfully and successfully busy producing dramatic works. He was granted printing privileges by George III and was appointed Music Master to Queen Charlotte, who was young and had recently been brought to England from a small German court. When young Mozart and his sister visited London in 1764 they became friends with John Bach, who later was to have a great influence on Wolfgang. Bach was enormously successful in London, composing not only serious opera but also lighter works for Covent Garden and the Vauxhall concerts, and managing at the same time to find time to work as a performing musician and concert manager. With Carl Friedrich Abel he started a series of subscription concerts, each man appearing as composer, conductor and soloist, first at Carlisle House, then Almack's Assembly Rooms and finally at Hanover Square Rooms. His fame by this time had travelled abroad and in 1772 he was invited to compose an opera for Mannheim, for the Elector's birthday celebrations—the ultimate compliment, since Mannheim was considered the most important musical centre in Europe at this time. For this occasion he wrote *Temistocle* (Themistocles). In 1778 he was commissioned to compose an opera for Paris and chose *Amadis des Gaules* (Amadis of the Gauls). Around this time, however, he began to suffer from professional set-backs, competition from another, more successful teacher called Johann Schroeter, and a decline of his own concert audiences. Continual worries undermined his health. He became very ill and died in 1782.

Johann Christian Bach; portrait attributed to Gainsborough (Liceo Musicale G. B. Martini: Photo Alinari)

14.2 When J. C. Bach was in Italy as a young man the symphony was already a reasonably independent form there—and no longer just a detached opera overture. The emphasis was on structure and thematic treatment of material, rather than orchestral colour or dance movement tunes. Bach wrote more than sixty symphonies, which were widely popular and had considerable influence on younger composers, including Mozart. On the whole his symphonies are in three movements, with a minuet or its equivalent as the last movement. His success is due in great part to the successful integration of German and Italian influences in his style, in much the same way, perhaps as his father's music is now seen as a happy fusion of Northern and Southern traditions.
Burney[1] wrote of him:

> J. C. Bach seems to have been the first composer who observed the law of *contrast*, as a *principle*. Before his time, contrast there frequently was, in the works of others; but it seems to have been accidental. Bach in his symphonies and other instrumental pieces, as well as in his songs, seldom failed, after a rapid and noisy passage, to introduce one that was slow and soothing. His symphonies seem infinitely more original than either his songs or harpsichord pieces, of which the harmony, mixture of wind instruments, and general richness and variety of accompaniment, are certainly the most prominent features.

This symphony in D is said to have been published in 1781. Alfred Einstein, in the introduction to his edition of the score, states, 'In freshness of invention and abundance of wit it is a real work for connoisseurs'; and he also maintains that the eighteenth-century connoisseur would have appreciated certain subtleties in the first movement that I'm afraid we probably miss today—the roundabout, devious return of the second subject in the recapitulation, the interplay of instruments in the crescendo of the coda and so on. We can however appreciate its direct appeal and spontaneity. It is scored for 2 oboes, bassoon, 2 horns, 2 trumpets, drums and strings. The trumpet and drum parts are found in a Dutch version of 1787 published by Schmidt. They are probably the publisher's own addition, but since it was customary for such additions to be encouraged we shall perform the symphony in this fuller orchestration.

Exercise

14.3 *Allegro con spirito*

Make a note of those features and characteristics in the opening 16 bars that you consider to be striking. What do you notice about tempo, rhythm, use of tutti and the general nature?

[1] *History*, vol. II.

Discussion

What strikes me at once is both its decisive nature and the fact that it is easily remembered due to its simple yet insistent rhythm and its repetitive nature. It is all built up on the tonic chord, and it commands absolute attention in a manner which we have come to expect in the opening of a symphony.

Notice the strong unison tutti followed by the unison motif on bassoon and strings accentuated at its final couple of beats each time by horns, trumpets, timpani and oboe. Notice the repetitive drumming bass over which the violin figuration is slurred

to give emphasis to the first beat and the appoggiatura. The subject itself can be divided up on best Wagenseil principle into three components

The bridge passage, which leads us to a 'present arms' cadence at bar 23 ready for an elegant second subject, is based on the second and subsequent bars, used sequentially in the bass part. This passage, slight and short, is not without vital charm. The bass part provides us with the harmonic and melodic movement. The first violins reiterate an accompaniment of repeated semiquavers, the whole orchestra emphasizes the harmony on the first beat of each bar, but the second violins interpolate something of their own, anticipating each first tutti beat by an audacious little run up—

first

then

then

Exercise

Listen carefully to the second subject (bars 24–43), and try to describe how its characteristics differ from those of the first subject. Consider its tonality, the nature of the melody and its layout.

Discussion

After a relatively occupied and busy bass line, what strikes one immediately and what, apart from the change of tonality (it is in the dominant, A major) provides the greatest contrast, is the serenity of this melody in the first violins, with its gently syncopated opening and its sustained accompaniment in the first bar. In the second bar the rests provide a breathing space and poise that we associate with Mozart. At the fourth bar we have a clichéd cadence

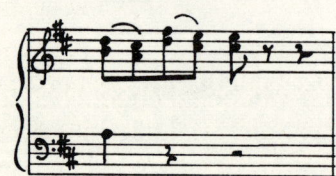

punctuated gently by oboes and horns linking this first phrase to a second, which, although starting similarly, extends in its fourth bar (bar 31) and introduces at bar 35 onward that second characteristic of our opening theme, the leaning appoggiatura quavers which push on the pace into semiquavers for a codetta to the exposition.

The development begins with a motif derived from the second subject treated antiphonally between wind and strings. Use is also made of an arpeggio figure derived from the same source and the appoggiatura figure of the opening. Sequences of syncopated arpeggios bring us to another 'present arms' in E minor. This introduces slight development of the second subject leading to a long pedal A, over which five bars of oboes and horns move magically around the dominant chord in preparation for the brilliant tutti recapitulation.

The most interesting feature in this recapitulation is perhaps the devious way in which we reach the second subject, this time, of course, in D major, via E major, E minor and A major (bars 100–12). The brief coda skilfully and humorously builds up to a climax which is resolved once again by unisons emphasizing a firm final cadence, and a typical one.

Exercise

How does Bach make use of his orchestral resources to achieve a climax and a sense of purpose and finality? (For example, does he use repetition, contrasted orchestration and strengthened resources?)

Discussion

You should have noticed:

(i) The repeated violin figurations.
(ii) The addition of wind to point the phrases.
(iii) The dovetailing of horn and trumpet parts.
(iv) The rests in the bass line which add point when the bass is then added.
(v) The repetitive harmonic scheme (mostly dominant and tonic) with accumulative orchestration.

The second movement is in G major (the 'flat' side of D major—it has one less sharp in its key signature). This movement also occurs in a different richer orchestration (with three 'clarinetti d'amore', extinct globe-belled clarinets) in the symphony of the Darmstadt copy of *Temistocle* (1772). It is in slow movement sonata form—that is sonata form without a development section, merely an exposition followed by a recapitulation. There is some effective and charming use of woodwind. The bassoon has a solo melody in octaves with the first violin at bars 5–8 (a combination usually ascribed to Haydn, since he makes such frequent and distinguished use of it), and there is another interesting entry at bars 17–18 where it plays a melodic and rhythmic role. Flutes have been substituted for the first movement oboes, and the economy with which they are used is effective. The scoring of the whole movement is more subdued—strings, bassoon and flutes, and when the flutes do enter they soar above the strings providing a new and restful tone colour.

In the recapitulation some considerable use is made of sustained woodwind, almost 'pedal' effects in bars 61–3 and 66–8 in the bassoon part, and again in bars 69–71 in the flute part. The scoring of this movement is lucid yet rich.

14.4 The spirit of the final rondo is perhaps nearest to Haydn—nearest anyway in humour and wit, in economy yet effectiveness of orchestration. Let's look at the opening. Of course, it seems obvious to us to play the rondo theme twice, the first time with strings and bassoon, the second time tutti; the first quietly, and the second loudly—obvious because of its effectiveness. Notice now the first episode uses the oboes and horns to point the peak of the phrases, and then at bar 37 onwards to answer the strings. There is not much harmonic variety, so it comes as a splendid surprise when the second episode plunges us without warning into the minor—something again that we take so much for granted now.

Exercise

To what do you attribute the vitality of this minor episode (bars 75–130)?

Discussion

Its drive is due to syncopated rhythms, and the contrast of imitative entries, unison passages and homophony.

I find this Finale extremely lively and attractive. There is some splendid antiphonal contrast at the very end.

Exercise

What do you think of this movement as a Finale? Does it balance the symphony as a whole? Is its simple form satisfactory?

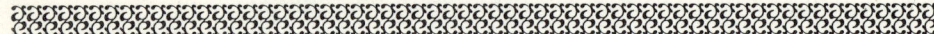

15.0 **CASE STUDY 6**

Rosetti: Symphony in G minor. 1787.

15.1 Franz Anton Rössler (or Rösler) was born around 1750 in Leitmeritz (fifty miles north of Prague) in northern Bohemia. Some confusion over the date and place of his birth exists—it is also given as 1745 in Nieměs. He became known later as Francesco Antonio Rosetti. There is confusion, also, concerning other facts about him, since there appear to have been no less than five musical Antonio Rosettis around at that time—for example a Milanese opera-composer, and a violinist at Esterháza whom Haydn met.

Our man went to school in Prague and then in 1763 to a Jesuit seminary in Kuttenberg. He did not finally take orders, and in 1773 he entered the service of Count Oettingen-Wallerstein at Wallerstein (sixty miles east of Stuttgart), first as double-bass player, and then in 1785 as Kapellmeister. Here he was responsible for the chapel music and music for feasts and celebrations. The count was well educated and widely travelled in Western Europe, and visiting artists and virtuosos at Wallerstein included Mozart, Punto, Hampeln and Echard. At Wallerstein Rosetti gained skill and technique in orchestral writing, and came to know the works of Haydn, Stamitz and Mozart.

By 1781 he was well known as a composer and was receiving many commissions, and was invited to Paris where his success was enormous. Here he also met Gluck and Piccinni. He wrote home to his employer glowing and colourful accounts of his experiences.

Now at last I am seeing all my dreams perfectly fulfilled! I don't lack sufficient acquaintances in the best households, and my *Musique* is performed more than that of masters ten times more worthy; I myself am popular with everyone from the Prince to the musician; my talent has every opportunity to grow better through the variety offered by the musical life of this place.

Paris, 25 January, 1782

One hears nothing but the symphonies of Haydn and——: dare I say it, Rosetti!—occasionally something by Ditters. . . .

Paris, 5 March 1782

In February 1782 the Mesure de France reported the *concert spirituel* 'began with a well-constructed symphony by M. Rosetti, which enhances considerably the reputation he has developed in this sphere'.

The Count Ernst was very pleased. Rosetti's last five years at Wallerstein, however, were full of ill-health and financial worries. Although he had become Kapellmeister in 1785 he didn't see eye to eye with the count over financial matters and eventually accepted the position of Kapellmeister to the Duke of Mecklenburg-Schwerin at Ludwigslust (sixty miles south-east of Hamburg). The position he left had become an important one. The repertoire of the chapel had become impressive, and concert items included works by the Mannheimers Stamitz, Cannabich and Toeschi as well as the Viennese composers and the North Germans like C. P. E. Bach and Franz Benda. The greater part of Rosetti's instrumental music was written in these years at Wallerstein.

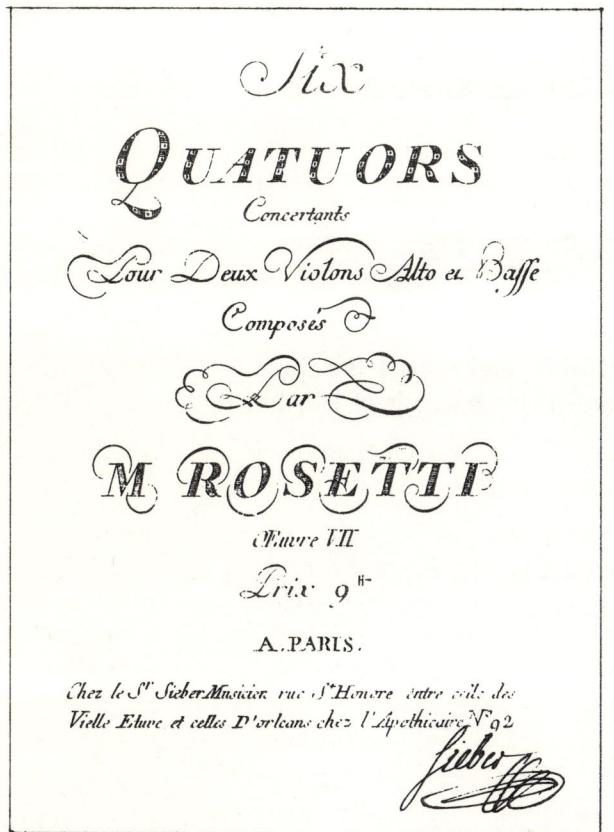

Title page of 'Six Quatuors Concertants Pour Deux Violons, Alto et Basse par M. Rosetti, Opus VII', Paris 1788 (Archiv für Kunst und Geschichte, Berlin)

The tradition at Ludwigslust, however, was mainly choral, and although the court was musical there was not the standard of orchestral playing or the same body of instrumentalists. Rosetti's contract stipulated that he should be in charge of all orchestral players and singers and direct all concerts in the concert hall and the chapel as well as compose music. His salary was more than triple that at Wallerstein. Although his health was now failing these last three years were most productive. In spite of lack of good singers and orchestral players he had such a flair for getting things going and was most industrious. He found the musical requirements of choir, soloists and orchestra at Ludwigslust liberated his ideas and gave him greater scope and freedom. Choral works such as *Winzerfest der Hirten* (Shepherds' Winter-feast), *Jesus in Gethsemane* and *Halleluja* were the result. On the strength of these works he was commissioned on Mozart's death in 1791 to compose a requiem for performance by the Prague national theatre orchestra in the St Nicholas church in Prague. This paved the way for another commission from Berlin for Princess Fredericka's marriage celebrations,[1] and in 1792 his oratorio *Jesus in Gethsemane* was performed in the royal chapel at Berlin. Altogether, these last years were happy due mainly to the good relationship with his employer and family. He died of some consumptive disease in 1792.

15.2 Apart from thirty-four symphonies Rosetti composed chamber music, an opera, two oratorios and some concertos. There is no doubt that Schubert as a schoolboy knew Rosetti's orchestral works, and may well have been influenced by them. In style Rosetti is often compared with Haydn. In his preface to the Denkmäler[2] edition, Oskar Kaul divides Rosetti's symphonies into three periods.

(i) Those in a tight form, and pre-Haydnesque—Symphonies 1–10.
(ii) Symphonies 11–22 including the six dedicated to the Prince of Oettingen-Wallerstein from Paris that were performed in the *concerts spirituels* of 1781 and 1782. These are characterized by more thematic development.
(iii) Symphonies 23–34 which reveal a greater security of technical handling.

Some of the first movement openings show the obvious influence of Stamitz and Mannheim in the rocketing arpeggio figures, although Rosetti did add a slow introduction to some.

Symphony in C (1781)

The minuet is typical of that of Haydn and Mozart, and indeed the final phrase is often repeated at the end of the sentence—a characteristic of Haydn also.

---

[1] Princess Fredericka, eldest daughter of King William II of Prussia, married Frederick, Duke of York, in Berlin in September 1791.

[2] *Denkmäler Deutscher Tonkunst XII* (i).

His slow movements have lyricism and poise.

Symphony in D (1780)

Finales often adopt the Austrian or Bohemian folk-like rondo although compared with the brief and tidy finales of Stamitz and his colleagues, those do tend to be unpredictable and capricious, as is the G minor finale. Another characteristic he shares with the Mannheimers is the way he uses dynamics such as *sforzandos* and crescendos.

Schubart described him as 'der beliebsten Tonsetzer unserer Zeit' (the best-loved composer of our time) and a critic in the Freiburg 'Beitrage zur Geschichte der Musik' (Contributions to the History of Music) of 1790 had this to say of him:

> It seems as if Rosetti wants to tread a solitary untrodden path—a path that without doubt being new and graceful should endure.

---

[1] Menuet fresco = 'open-air' minuet.

pia }
po } = *piano* = quietly

cal = *calando* = dying away, getting quieter

for = *forte* = loudly

15.3 The symphony no. 29 in G minor was composed in March 1782 at Wallerstein. It is scored for strings, 1 flute, 2 oboes and bassoon and 2 horns. There are three other well-known symphonies in G minor; Haydn no. 39 (*c.* 1768), Mozart no. 25, K.183 (1773), and Mozart no. 40, K.550 (1788) and also one by J. C. Bach (op. 6 no. 6). You will be discussing these in the next block of units. There is certainly a strange link between these works besides the similarity of key.

Vivace

The first movement opens in a pregnant and mysterious way.

Exercise

Do you agree? If so, why?

Discussion

The following points surely contribute towards it.
  (i) The fragmentary nature of the opening theme and its repetitive use.
  (ii) The sparse scoring of the opening, with the first violins accompanied only by second violin and viola.
  (iii) The piano, and later pianissimo dynamic.
  (iv) The use of repeated notes leaning towards a long appoggiatura.

After the initial eleven bars there is an effective moment at the repetition of the opening when the low notes of 'cellos and bassoons give an added depth—and six bars later where the double bass joins in to give an even greater depth. The tension builds up as woodwind joins in and the whole orchestra cadences on a D major chord, followed by a pause.

Exercise

Play the opening until bar 52 and comment on what happens in bars 30 onwards.

Discussion

The new idea that enters immediately after the pause in bar 29 is probably the bridge passage, although it begins immediately in the new key, B♭ major, the relative major to G minor, and the key of the second subject to come.

This new motif at bar 30 is a descending figure tossed between first violins and oboe, and second violins and oboe. The original restless mood of the opening is maintained by the repeated quavers in the accompaniment, and the touches of chromaticism in the melodic line. The second subject, also in B♭, is distinguished by its contrasting nature (it is gentle and sweet) but it again makes use of that slightly disconcerting motif

Later moments like bars 71–73

are emotionally akin to the Mozart G minor symphonies. The exposition is repeated.

Exercise

Play the movement over and follow the score and then comment on the development section.

Discussion

The development starts directly in B♭ minor and makes much use of the original  figure, moving quickly through keys in a way that we have not previously encountered. The section is perhaps a little disappointing in that it makes no reference to the several other themes and rhythmic figures introduced in the exposition.

The recapitulation at bar 143 is encountered in a subtle and delightful way, emerging from the development quietly and naturally after we have been anticipating it because of the play on that opening motive. We know it has at last arrived because of confirmation in the bass by adding just that touch of security and emphasis.

The second subject group reappears surprisingly suddenly in G major, and continues quite happily in this key until it plunges back into G minor at bar 192. The opposition of G minor and G major here and in the last movement illustrates a characteristic we had noticed in Wagenseil and which we find again in Schubert.

15.4 *Menuet Fresco—Allegretto*

This second movement minuet and trio is unusually placed, preceding the slow movement. In fact this is a disposition of movements we don't find often at this time. It is characterized by a certain chromaticism and the dance-like lilt of the Haydnesque minuet. Notice the way the first sentence is extended to twelve bars by a four-bar afterthought. In the trio the oboe solo (doubled by first violins, accompanied by pizzicato strings and over a bass pedal) is particularly charming with its stressed appoggiaturas.

After the trio the minuet is repeated *da capo* (from the beginning) to make a broad ternary structure.

15.5 *Andante ma Allegretto*

In this broadly ternary movement we can see progress towards a more developmental slow movement style. Although of an extemporary nature the movement stresses the increasing importance of development of material. I find the approach to the recapitulation (up to bar 74) particularly well prepared, and would also like to draw your attention to Rosetti's treatment of the bass part, which is both economical and telling, and almost Schubertian in places.

15.6 *Allegro Scherzante*

This last movement is much more substantial than previous finales we have looked at. It is a delightful rondo with many touches of humour—not least the sudden key changes and the indecisive approach at bars 92–7, and again at bars 114–22.

This is a procrastinating device that we have grown used to with Haydn, but is none the less most teasing. The major episode (really the minor theme transposed) provides contrast in both key and sonority with oboe and flute solos. The last statement of the rondo theme is preceded by a skilful orchestral build-up. If you just look at the eight bars preceding the major change (bar 209) you can see how simple devices complement each other to produce a continuous build-up of sound. Flute and oboes sustain the harmony above. Horns and lower strings repeat it with a rhythmic motif that is emphatic and yet at the same time lets the air in:

—the violins have powerful split chords in between with just a little quaver up-beat in the second violin part to give the whole a kick of impetus.

Exercise

In looking at this symphony as a whole, can you list some of the features illustrating the progress it has made by comparison with the early case studies? (For example: length; form; mood; orchestration; performance directions.)

Discussion

I hope you mentioned some of the following points.

    (i) It is longer and altogether more substantial.
   (ii) Internal organization of material is toward a more developmental form.
  (iii) It is in four fully independent movements.
  (iv) The orchestration stipulated is exact.
   (v) It contains a certain amount of emotion and subjectivity.
  (vi) It contains humour.
 (vii) String, wind and horn parts are characteristic of the nature of particular instruments.
(viii) The bass line plays a new role and is used with economy and meaning.
  (ix) Dynamics, phrasing and other interpretative directions are included and precisely thought out.

APPENDIX

Record 4: Contents

Side 1:

Sammartini: Symphony in G major, first movement
Wagenseil: Symphony in D major, first movement
Stamitz: Symphony in E♭ major, first movement
C. P. E. Bach: Symphony in D major

Side 2:

J. C. Bach: Symphony in D major op. 18 no. 4
Rosetti: Symphony in G minor

List of Chief Composers of Symphonies

ABEL, Carl Friedrich (1723–87), London
ARNE, Thomas (1710–78), London
ASPLMAYR, Franz (c. 1721–86), Vienna
BACH, Carl Philipp Emanuel (1714–88), Berlin
BACH, Johann Christian (1735–82), London
BECK, Franz (1730–1809), Mannheim, Bordeaux
BENDA, Franz (1709–86), Berlin
BENDA, Georg (1722–95), Berlin
BOCCHERINI, Luigi (1743–1805), Paris
BOYCE, William (1710–79), London
CAMBINI, Giovanni Giuseppe (1746–1825), Paris
CANNABICH, Christian (1731–98), Mannheim
COLLETT, John (fl. 1765), London
DANZI, Franz (1763–1826), Mannheim
DELLER, Johann Florian (1729–73), Stuttgart, Munich
DITTERS, Karl (von Dittersdorf) (1739–99), Vienna
EBERL, Anton (c. 1765–1807), Vienna, St. Petersburg
EICHNER, Ernst (1740–77), Mannheim
FILTZ, Anton (c. 1730–60), Mannheim
FISHER, John (1744–1806), London
FRÄNZEL, Ignaz (1736–1811), Mannheim
GALUPPI, Baldassare (1706–85), Venice
GASSMAN, Florian Leopold (1729–74), Vienna
GOSSEC, François Joseph (1734–1829), Paris
GRAUN, Carl Heinrich (1704–59), Berlin
GRAUN, Johann Gottlieb (1703–71), Berlin
GUILLEMAIN, Louis-Gabriel (1705–70), Paris
HASSE, Johann Adolf (1699–1783), Dresden
HAYDN, Franz Joseph (1732–1809), Esterházy, Vienna
HAYDN, Johann Michael (1737–1806), Vienna
HOFFMANN, Leopold (c. 1730–93), Vienna
HOLZBAUER, Ignaz (1709–83), Mannheim
JOMMELLI, Niccolò (1714–74), Rome, Stuttgart
KOZELUH, Leopold Anton (1752–1818), Vienna
MARSH, John (1752–1828), London
MARTIN, François (1727–57), Paris
MONN, Georg Matthias (1717–50), Vienna
MOZART, Wolfgang Amadeus (1756–91), Vienna
d'ORDOÑEZ (1734–86), Vienna

PAISIELLO, Giovanni (1740–1816), Naples
PICCINNI, Niccolò (1728–1800), Naples, Rome, Paris
PLEYEL, Ignaz Joseph (1757–1831), Paris, London, Vienna
PUGNANI, Gaetano (1731–98), Turin
RICHTER, Franz Xaver (1709–89), Mannheim, Strasbourg
ROSETTI, Franz Anton (c. 1750–92), Wallerstein, Ludwigslust
SACCHINI, Antonio (1730–86), Naples, Rome, Venice, London, Paris
SAMMARTINI, Giovanni Battista (1698–1775), Milan
SCHENK, Johann (1753–1836), Vienna
SCHOBERT, Johann (c. 1720–67), Paris
STAMITZ, Johann (1717–57), Mannheim
STAMITZ, Karl (1745–1801), Mannheim, Paris, London
STARZER, Josef (1726–87), Vienna, St. Petersburg
TOESCHI, Carlo Giuseppe (1722/4–88), Mannheim
VAŇHAL (or Wanhal), Jan (1739–1813), Vienna
WAGENSEIL, Georg Christoph (1715–77), Vienna
WERNER, Gregor Joseph (c. 1695–1766), Esterházy
ZARTH (or Tzarth), Georg (1708–78), Mannheim

Recordings Currently Available (1973)

C. P. E. BACH

Symphony in E minor (W177, 1756)   English Chamber Orchestra/Leppard 6833035   SAL3689

6 Symphonies (W182, 1773), nos 2, 3, 5.   English Chamber Orchestra/Leppard   SAL3689

4 Symphonies (W183)   English Chamber Orchestra/Leppard   SAL3701
Munich Bach Orchestra/Richter   2533050
Ars Redivivia/Munchinger   1100576
Little Orchestra of London/Jones   H711806

6 Symphonies (W182)   No. 1   Munich Bach Orchestra/Richter   SAWT9420
No. 2   St Martin's Academy/Marriner   SDD336
No. 3   Amsterdam Chamber Orchestra/Rieu   SAWT 9447
2 sides: Little Orchestra of London/Jones   H71180

J. C. BACH

Symphonies, op. 3 nos. 1–6   2 sides: St Martin's Academy/Marriner   6500 11S

Symphonies: op. 6 no. 6 in G minor   New Philharmonia/Leppard   SAL3685
op. 9 no. 1 in B♭   New Philharmonia/Leppard   SAL3685
op. 9 no. 2 in E♭   English Chamber Orchestra/Bonynge   SXL 6397
op. 9 no. 3 in B♭   Hurwitz Chamber Orchestra/Hurwitz   SOL 317
op. 18 nos. 1–6:
1, 2, 4   English Chamber Orchestra/Davis   SOL 317
2   Munich Bach Orchestra/Richter   SAWT 9420
2   New Philharmonia/Leppard   SAL3685
5   English Chamber Orchestra/Hurwitz   SDD147
5   Frankfurt Bach Orchestra/Stephani   3C308

WILLIAM BOYCE

8 Symphonies (*c.* 1750)
1–8   Württembêrg Chamber Orchestra/Faerber   TV34 133S
1–8   Solisti di Zagreb/Janigro   HM23SD
1, 4   English Chamber Orchestra/Hurwitz   SDD147

J. M. HAYDN

Symphony No. 16 (+ Mozart's Intro.) (formerly Mozart no. 37) Little Orchestra of London/Jones   GSGC 14131
Symphony No. 20   Hungarian Chamber Orchestra/Tatrai   SLPX 1248
Symphony No. 27   Hungarian Chamber Orchestra/Tatrai   SLPX 11462
English Chamber Orchestra/Mackerras   2533 074
Symphony No. 33   Little Orchestra of London/Jones   GSGC 14131
Symphony No. 44   Budapest Philharmonic Orchestra/Erdelyi   SLPX 1264
Symphony in D (1777) (Turkish Suite for Voltaire's 'Zaire')   English Chamber Orchestra/Mackerras   2533 074

G. B. SAMMARTINI

Symphonies 1, 3, 6, 13, 16, 19   Camden Chamber Orchestra/Lubbock   BACH 1705

Acknowledgements

Grateful acknowledgement is made for use of material in these units as follows:

Text

J. M. Dent & Sons Ltd. for H. T. David and A. Mendel (eds.) *The Bach Reader*; Faber and Faber Ltd. for Friedrich Blume, *Classic and Romantic Music*; Hutchinson & Co Ltd. for Thurston Dart, *The Interpretation of Music*; Macmillan & Co. Ltd. for G. Grove, *A Dictionary of Music and Musicians*.

Illustrations

Archiv für Kunst und Geschichte, Berlin: *pp 16 and 58*; Barenreiter & Company: *p. 46*; Burgermeisteramt der Stadt Schwetzingen: *p. 28* (lower); Fotofast: *p. 53*; Landesbildstelle, Baden: *pp 19, 25, 27* (*lower*), *28* (*upper*) *and 29*; Mansell Collection: *pp 17, 18, 34 and 72*; National Gallery, London: *p. 23*; National Library, Budapest: *p. 67*; Österreichische Nationalbibliothek Musiksammlung: *p. 59*; Oxford University Press: *p. 45*; Radio Times Hulton Picture Library: 26 (lower); Reissmuseum Mannheim, Photo Landesdenkmalamt, Baden-Württemberg: *p. 26* (*upper*) *and 27* (*upper*); State Library of Czech Socialist Republic: *p. 63*.

The Development of Instruments and their Music

Block 1	*The Baroque Organ and Bach Organ Music*
Unit 1	The Baroque Organ
2	Bach Organ Music
3	The Baroque Organ: Scores Bach Organ Music

Block 2	*Baroque Instrumental Music*
4, 5, 6	Baroque Instrumental Music I: People, Instruments and the Continuo
7, 8, 9	Baroque Instrumental Music II: Suite, Sonata and Concerto
10	Baroque Instrumental Music: Scores
11	Baroque Instrumental Music: Scores

Block 3	*The Rise of the Symphony*
12, 13	The Rise of the Symphony I
14a	The Rise of the Symphony I: Scores A
14b	The Rise of the Symphony I: Scores B
15, 16	The Rise of the Symphony II
17a	The Rise of the Symphony II: Scores A
17b	The Rise of the Symphony II: Scores B

Block 4	*The Rise of the String Quartet*
18	The Rise of the String Quartet
19	The Rise of the String Quartet: Scores

Block 5	*From Classical to Romantic Keyboard Music*
20, 21, 22	From Classical to Romantic Keyboard Music

Block 6	*Modern Music*
23, 24, 25	Twentieth-Century Music 1900–1945
26	Twentieth-Century Music 1900–1945: Scores
27, 28, 29	Contemporary Music: Case Studies I
30	Music and Society Today
31, 32	Contemporary Music: Case Studies II